Childh

Helmet
Stump City Two

Mike Quigley

2008

Childhood without a Helmet

TABLE OF CONTENTS

Prologue   xi
Stuffed Chairs   I
Mrs. Wickham   7
The Grandparents' House   9
Tony Leonti   II
Kimak Potatoes   15
Mr. O'Hara's Horse   17
Halloween   19
Two Wheeled Excitement   21
The Quarry Dump   25
Paint Job   27
Mr. Hanville's Great Rides   33
School Lunch   37
First Haircut   39
Plums Gone Wild   43
Pickup Games   47
Field Days at the American Legion   49
Poncho Verses the Legion Auction   51
The Boob Tube Affects Me   57
Dirt Clods and Asbestos Shingles   63
Sledding Makes an Impression   67
Many are Called, But...   71
Grapes of Wrath   75
Sledding at Beaver Meadow   81
Milk by the Gallons   85
Rat Shoot   91
Gone Fishing   95

Buggy Ride	105
Beaver Meadow: Part II	117
Fooled by Mr. Pinker	121
The Boob Tube Affects Me: Part II	125
The O'Hara Home	133
Roberta Staples and King	139
Paper Boy	143
Wine into Water	149
Broken Glasses	153
Magazine Boy	159
Almost a Heart Attack Dummy	165
Gravity Works	171
The Blind Teaching the Blind	177
Like Shooting Fish in a Barrel	181
Chopping More than Weeds	183
Boy Scouts and Doughnuts	189
Unfriendly Fire	195
Beaver Meadow: Part III	199
Courts and High Jumping	203
Bad Snowball	205
Huck and Tom Raft Again	211
Chubby Trout	217
Winter at Sheldon Pond	223
Bending Branches	227
The Sheridan Boys	231
Bus Racing	233
The Colonial Theatre	237
Clift Park	239
From Berry Picking to Walking the Plank	243
Confusing Times	253

PROLOGUE

Many of the adventures I lived through while growing up in a small community were not mentioned in **Stump City**. Instead, I centered recollections on the family and didn't wander too much away from what happened in or near the house.

It's now time to widen the tale to include most of what happened once I was allowed to gradually venture further from home without Mom or Dad close by to keep an eye on me. I say "most" because I'm not sure if the statute of limitations has passed, and I'm getting too old to spend time in Auburn Prison.

As it was in **Stump City**, most of what I tell is the truth, but with a wee bit of Irish exaggeration. Further, I realize that adding years to recollections tends to strain the memory part of our brains—sometimes turning facts almost to the point of fiction.

Stump City told how I escaped from the enclosed front yard and almost drove Mom to distraction until she figured out how I was getting out.

Those short trips away from the wooden picket fenced area were fun for me, but I never wanted to wander too far from home. There were many unknown things outside the fenced area that frightened me, especially once the sun started to go down, shadows started to appear, and strange noises came out of the increasing darkness.

I began traveling off our property on my own when I was about four. Mom and Dad decided that I was old enough to visit neighbors who lived close by without drifting into the woods, drowning in Skaneateles Creek, getting chewed up by a neighbor's dog, or being kidnapped by Gypsies.

If you are a youngster, your mom might want you to put on a helmet when you read parts of the book. If you are getting on in years, you might wonder how you and I survived some of the things we did back when helmets were only worn by soldiers and some sissy players of sports requiring curved sticks or a strangely shaped ball.

The tales will appear in chronological order starting in 1950 and ending in 1960. I know some of the events will not be in order because I've plain forgotten exactly when they happened.

That's enough. It's time to roll up my sleeves and start pounding the keyboard...

STUFFED CHAIRS

One of my first solo missions was to Helen and John McEneny's house, located all of fifty feet from our home. Mom needed a cup of sugar for something she was going to bake later in the day. She handed me the cup, unhooked the safety catch near the top of the kitchen door, and sent me on my way.

Halfway there, sensing someone was watching me, I turned my head back toward home. Mom was standing on the porch and waving. I waved back and continued on my journey.

I strolled up the sidewalk, knocked on the kitchen door, and waited for Mrs. McEneny to answer. I knew it wouldn't be Mr. McEneny coming to the door because he never answered it if his wife was home. If he was alone and a Yankee game was on the radio, not even Father McMahon would dare pay a visit because Mr. McEneny might just slip up and let out a curse word or two while mumbling something about his concentration on the game being broken.

Mrs. McEneny opened the door and said, "Why, Michael, how are you? After looking behind me and not seeing Mom or Dad, she added, "And where might your parents be?"

"I'm fine, Mrs. McEneny. Mom sent me over all by myself to get a cup of sugar." I tried to sound grownup when I said it.

She smiled and held the screen door open to let me in.

"Would you like to sit yourself down and have a cookie and a glass of milk while we chatter a bit?"

I quickly nodded my head up and down and sat.

While she got the milk from the ice box and the cookie from the jar, she made small talk about the weather and the family's health.

She noticed I was looking around and said, "Rose isn't here right now, Michael. She's at a friend's house."

Rose was their only child. She was spoiled, but in a nice way. I always had fun with her.

"I was hoping she would be here," I answered and kept an eye on the cookie. Mrs. McEneny was a very good baker.

While I ate, I made sure to watch my manners and not talk with my mouth full.

I heard Mr. McEneny slowly walking into the kitchen and looked up as he made a slight nod in my direction.

I nodded back.

He smiled and winked.

I winked back with a smile on my face.

He was wearing his usual blue work pants and white tee shirt with the pants held up by suspenders. His slippered feet always scuffed the floor a bit as if he didn't want to let them leave the earth by any more than the minimum required to move.

Mr. McEneny was retired from Waterbury Felt Company where he had worked for many years. He had meaty hands just like his brother, Big Jim, but his belly wasn't nearly the size of Big Jim's. I think that was because Big Jim liked his Genesee beer a little more than John did.

He turned to his wife and said, "Woman, If it isn't much trouble, I'd like a cup of tea and one of your grand cookies. I'll take it in the living room, if you don't mind."

He turned to me knowing that his order would be filled and said, "Michael, come on into the living room and sit for a bit."

He said this with the same motion of his hand he used when he wanted his workers to do his bidding while managing them at the felt company. The hand said, "Come now. I don't have time to dilly-dally."

I followed him in and took a seat on the high foot stool. It had been my spot to sit and listen since I was old enough to walk. I now noticed that if I stretched, my toes could touch the floor.

I watched as he plopped himself down in his over-stuffed chair. His feet always rose a few inches off the floor when his back hit the rear of the chair just like Grandpa Quigley's did.

His beloved radio was within reach and pointed in his direction. The other chair in the room was for his wife and matched his. It wasn't nearly as worn but had a well-used look about it.

We made polite to one another until Mrs. McEneny came in with his tea and cookie. She placed them on the stand between the two chairs.

She liked to make her husband feel like he was in charge, but from what I had learned from listening in to her talking with Mom, she really ruled the roost. She was a smart little woman.

She sat down in her chair and moved around as if to try and make herself comfortable. She twitched from one side of her bottom to the other with the worry lines on her face working overtime.

"John," she said with a frown and seriousness, "T'is a fact that me chair is getting uncomfortable." After a pause and with the frown still on her face, she added, "Given the hours you have yourself planted in yours, yours must be mighty uncomfortable. Why, I don't know how you can concentrate on a Yankee game with all the lumps poking you here and there."

Mr. McEneny suddenly developed some worry lines on his forehead while he was thinking about what she had said and replied, "Why, Helen, I do believe you be right. I do seem to be fidgeting more than I did twenty odd years ago when we got the chairs."

They were now both twitching their bottoms.

She nodded slowly, paused, and said, "John, I'd be guessing that you'd be wanting a nice new one to feel comfortable in. And t'is true that mine is not much better."

After another pause that wasn't long enough for him to reply, she added, "Come to think of it, I did see an advertisement in yesterday's paper for Rondina's Furniture Store. They be having a big sale this weekend."

As if the idea of his very own making entered his head, he said, "Woman, I think it be time for two new chairs. I don't want an argument about the cost. We'll be off to Auburn tomorrow. And, there won't be another word about it."

Mrs. McEneny looked my way with a slight smile on her face. She had recently complained to Mom about the worn out chairs when she came over for a visit.

I soon said that I must be going back home because Mom didn't want me to stay long.

I said my good-bye to Mr. McEneny.

He waved a hand at me and didn't say anything because his mouth was full of cookie.

Mrs. McEneny walked into the kitchen with me and got a cup of sugar.

"Michael, t'is good that you came over. You put him in a good frame of mind for me."

During this and future visits, she taught me a thing or two on the workings going on in a woman's mind. I started to wonder if Mom and my sister were doing the same to me.

While I was walking home, I saw Mom looking at me out the side kitchen window. She was keeping an eye out for me and making sure I didn't wander off in the wrong direction. It made me feel good inside to know that she was. But at the same time, I wanted her to trust and not hover over me.

After a few more successful trips to the McEneny's, Mom stopped looking out the window and let me visit other neighbors.

MRS. WICKHAM

Mrs. Wickham lived on the corner of our street and Stump Road. She was a quiet woman who mainly kept to herself. Her husband, Pete, died a few years earlier. He was a carpenter and made many beautiful pieces of furniture for their home.

Mom visited her on occasion. She'd walk the short distance to her house with my sister, Terry, and me in tow while she carried our baby sister, Pat. It was too short a walk to bother with the big wheeled, black baby carriage.

Mrs. Wickham always invited us in and we'd sit at her kitchen table. She'd offer us children a snack to keep us occupied while she talked to Mom. She never had any children of her own but knew how to keep them peaceful.

We weren't allowed to venture into her living room, but I could see it from the kitchen. She had a beautiful lamp with a stained glass shade sitting in front of her picture window on a table her husband had made. All her furniture was polished and dust wasn't allowed.

Mrs. Wickham's first name was Mame. She was tall, very thin, kept her gray hair in a bun, and always wore old clothes around the house during the planting and growing seasons because she spent much of the good weather tending to her beautiful flower gardens and her large vegetable plot.

The garden areas were fenced in to keep out kids, chickens, cats, and dogs. She fussed over her gardens like a movie star worried over her makeup. Flowers were constantly in bloom from early spring to late fall. Once in a while, if she was in real good humor or thought of it, she'd give Mom a bunch to take home.

I liked to venture alone to her house. After I said a polite greeting and she returned with one of her own, I'd put my hands on the top of her fence and watch through the pickets as she worked in the gardens. She was constantly killing weeds and wouldn't stop to talk to me. Her hoe flew up and down in smooth motions never touching her beloved flowers. Every time the hoe hit the dirt, her oversized straw hat bowed down almost to her nose and the skin on her bony arms did a slight jiggle. There was a smooth, long-practiced rhythm to her hoeing.

I loved the colors in her gardens. She even had flowers growing around her one-seater outhouse. In the right season, purple morning glories grew up trellises leaving only the door uncovered in brilliant purple. It was by far the fanciest outhouse in Stump City,

She knew I liked and appreciated her flowers, so she put up with me as long as I kept quiet and didn't distract her aim with the hoe.

When I got through watching her I'd say, "Have a good afternoon, Mrs. Wickham."

Her only response would be a nod of her head, which made her straw hat give an extra nod as she continued working without breaking stride.

THE GRANDPARENTS' HOUSE

Mom eventually trusted me enough to let me go alone to Grandma and Grandpa's house on Stump Road.

If it was the right time in the morning, I'd see Mrs. Cashin sitting in the outhouse reading some magazine with the door open for ventilation. When she noticed me walking up the road, I'd wave to her and she'd always wave back and resume reading.

I never thought much about seeing her like that. She didn't make much of it either.

If the weather was good, Grandma Quigley sat on the front porch in her wicker wheelchair. The thing seemed to be always holding her back from getting up. She'd give me a crooked smile from her half paralyzed mouth when she saw me coming.

I'd sit next to her in an old, green metal lawn chair and rock back and forth as I talked to her. It was a one-sided conversation because Grandma had a stroke before I was born and couldn't talk well. Aunt Mary understood "Grandma Language" better than anyone else, so if she was around and not busy, she'd tell me what Grandma was saying.

When Aunt Mary was in a kind mood and thought about it, she'd give me a cookie. I remembered to be very polite around her because one wrong word or movement could result in a scolding. She always seemed to be looking for something to criticize, and it was a rare event for her not to find some fault with my behavior. I tried very hard not to give her a reason to scold me and quickly learned that it was good to sit very still and not say much when she was outside with Grandma and me.

If Grandma and I were alone, I'd chatter away and she'd listen. She liked to hear me talk. She'd either nod or mumble something to let me know that she was paying attention to what I was saying.

After the visit, I'd say good-by, give her a hug and kiss, and wave back at her as I went down the street. She'd nod, give a try at a crooked smile, and lift a hand an inch off the wheelchair arm to give me a very weak wave.

TONY LEONTI

Stump City only had twenty houses, but there were plenty of kids around. The problem was, they were all either older or younger than me. The older ones were already in school and the younger ones were either in diapers or just out of them.

Pete Cashin and Davy Walton were about two years older than me, and I considered them to be big kids. They were already in second grade. I didn't know them very well and only hung around with them when they weren't busy doing something together or finished with their daily chores.

Things changed once I started school. I met Tony Leonti in kindergarten. He lived about a mile west of Stump City on Depot Road.

One day Tony's mom let him walk all the way to our house after school to play with me. We had a great time on the swing and in the sandbox. Mom had a snack for us too.

At twenty-to-five, Tony said that he had to leave. His Mom wanted him home before the five o'clock train whistle blew on the roof of the Waterbury Felt Company signaling to the workers another day of making blankets was done.

He thanked Mom, said "so long" to me, and took off up our road towards his home at a slow trot.

The next day on the bus, I asked him if he made it home on time. He said he got back home with a few minutes to spare.

If Tony could do it, why couldn't I?

I asked Mom if it was okay for me to walk to Tony's. She wasn't happy about me walking all that way, but said that if I got home by the time the whistle blew, it would be all right with her.

She told me more than once to make sure I was home just before five, walk facing the traffic, and not go into the cow pasture known as Beaver Meadow because Mr. Peters always kept a big, mean bull there to keep the heifers happy.

After school the following day, I walked to Tony's. It was warm, and I had a little sweat beading on my face by the time I went up, down, and up the hills to get there. I did see heifers in the pasture, but didn't know how to tell if one of them was a bull.

Tony lived out in the country and had all kinds of things to do in the small woods behind his house. Tony and I had great fun. The time flew by.

We were in the middle of playing cowboys and Indians when I heard the five o'clock whistle blasting in the distance. I stopped dead in my tracks and came back to the real world with a jolt. What was going to happen to me when I got home? After all, Mom's serious tone was a warning to be home before the whistle blew.

I said a quick word or two in Tony's direction as I started running towards home. It was at least five-after-five when I got back to the edge of Stump City. During the panic run-time towards home, my overactive imagination took over. I thought up many terrible things that could happen to me for punishment.

I was getting close to my grandparents' house when I looked up and saw Mom walking up the street towards me.

Because of the thoughts I had been thinking, I blurted out, "Mom, don't hit me. Please don't hit me."

I kept saying it over and over again as I slowly got closer to her.

When I was within arms' reach, she grabbed me by the wrist, leaned over, and put her mouth to my ear. She whispered, "I wasn't going to spank you, but after all that fuss and noise and all the neighbors listening, you will get it when you are home!"

Dad was back from work and heard my animal like screaming as Mom pulled me along down our road. He came out onto the porch and asked Mom what was going on.

Mom said, "Michael has been crying and fussing all the way down Stump Road. All the neighbors must think we constantly whip the poor child. I'm so embarrassed!"

Dad turned his face to me and said, "Well, I think you'd better get something to cry about."

He took my hand and led me into the kitchen. He then took off his belt, laid me over his knee, and gave me three solid whacks across the bottom.

It was my first of several meetings with the belt.

Finishing the job, he said, "Now get upstairs and think about what you have done. There'll be no supper for you tonight."

I lay in bed on my stomach because the other side hurt. What hurt even more was realizing I had put up such a fuss in front of so many people.

It was many years before I came home past Mom or Dad's appointed time, and the sound of the Waterbury Whistle took on new meaning for me every time I heard it.

KIMAK POTATOES

Andy Kimak and his very old father lived at the end of our street. Andy owned the Southern Star Restaurant, a very popular place a mile west of Auburn. He spent most of his waking hours every day except Mondays working at the restaurant and wasn't home much.

Old Mr. Kimak spoke broken English and was hard to understand. He was so skinny that a decent gust of wind could easily blow him over if he wasn't permanently hunched forward as if he was constantly walking against one. He didn't leave the property much and spent his time puttering around the house and yard or napping in a chair by the back door.

I was playing kick-the-can and made it to the end of our street without putting it in a ditch, a major accomplishment. I happened to look up and saw Old Mr. Kimak sitting in a chair next to the garage. There was a large metal machine right next to his chair and a huge container filled with potatoes soaking in water.

I yelled, "Good morning, Mr. Kimak. How are you feeling today?"

I said this to be polite and also because I knew that he'd been ailing lately.

He replied with a string of broken English I couldn't understand. I did hear him say "better" at one point.

I said, "Glad to hear it, Mr. Kimak."

He gestured for me to come closer.

I looked at the machine. It had an electrical cord running from it to the backdoor of the house. On one end there was a hole leading to a big metal area. On the other end was another hole with a large bucket half filled with clean water placed underneath it.

Mr. Kimak saw that I looked puzzled. He gestured with a well-veined hand for me to pick up a potato and pointed to the hole.

As I went to put it in, he turned on the machine. It made a soft whooshing sound. I dropped the potato into the hole and it came out the other end completely peeled.

I spent a good fifteen minutes feeding the machine while Mr. Kimak picked up and examined each one as it dropped into the bucket of water. If he saw any skins or eyes, he cut them off with a knife.

When we were done, I said, "Thank you for letting me help. It was fun."

He smiled at me and said something that I didn't understand. I waved to him as I started kicking the can back towards home.

I told Mom about the machine and how fast it peeled potatoes.

She said, "I could use one of those around here with all the spuds we eat. It would give me some extra time to do other things around the house."

MR. O'HARA'S HORSE

We were eating supper one evening and Dad announced he was going to let Mr. O'Hara fence in our small lot behind the house except for the area Dad used for his vegetable garden. Mr. O'Hara's pony, Pal, and his small milking cow, Betsey, needed more room to graze, and it would be a good way to keep the weeds down in the field.

I wasn't happy about this plan because I liked to crawl around in the tall grass pretending I was a soldier sneaking up on Germans. It was great fun until a mouse or a snake scared me half out of my mind. I'd get up in a hurry and run back to the house.

Pal and Betsey weren't in the field all the time, but when they were, I learned to stay far away from Pal. He had a nasty disposition and either chased me out of the field or reached over the fence, if I got too close to it, and tried to take a chunk out of me. He was the only flesh eating horse I even ran across.

Once in awhile I'd see Mr. O'Hara leading Pal up or down the streets on a leash attached to a halter. He'd stop and talk to folks and hold the rope like someone else would hold a leash attached to a dog. Pal would stand there and not move anything except his tail.

Pal certainly didn't act like a well-trained dog when Mr. O'Hara wasn't around.

Word spread around Stump City that Mr. O'Hara took Pal to Rodak's one night and led him right up to the bar. He ordered a beer for himself and a bucket of the same for Pal. It would have been a wonderful sight to see them both staggering home. I'm sorry I missed it.

HALLOWEEN

Halloween was a fearful time for me as a youngster. Before I was old enough to go trick or treating, I'd be in the kitchen when kids knocked on the door. I quickly learned to hide in the bottom of the huge cupboard in the kitchen until the scary creatures got their treats, and I heard the door close behind them.

When I was old enough to go out with other kids, I got dressed up, Mom armed me with a paper bag and a bar of soap, and I was off.

The most fun was soaping windows of those neighbors who weren't home or didn't give us much candy. Often someone would come out and either yell at or chase us. My heart pounded with both fear and excitement as I ran away.

I never collected much candy but had a good time. I always made sure to stay close to the older kids because I was afraid something would jump out at me. I constantly looked over my shoulder expecting to see some hideous monster reaching out with a clawed hand to latch onto me and rip me to shreds.

TWO WHEELED EXCITEMENT

At the age of four, I liked to pretend that I was a famous race car driver when I rode my tricycle on the street in front of our house. I pedaled as fast as I could and sometimes make turns too quick tipping over the tricycle. This usually added a few more cuts and bruises to my collection.

I was in the middle of a big race with another pretend driver, when Davey Walton and Pete Cashin rode up on their big boy two-wheelers.

Davey looked at Pete and said, "Pete, don't you think it's time for Mike to learn how to ride a big guy bike?"

"I sure do." Pete replied with a smile.

I knew something was up and started to get nervous.

"What do you mean? I'm too small to reach the pedals on your bikes."

Pete said, "Heck, I was younger than you when I first learned."

"So was I," said Davey. "Come up to the top of the hill and we will give you a lesson."

I didn't want anything to do with this, but didn't want them to know I was scared either.

I hesitated before I said, "Okay, but only one lesson."

When we got to the top of the hill, Pete turned his beat up bike so it was facing downhill.

He said, "I'll help you get on, steady the bike for you, and let you try for a few feet. We will be on either side to keep you from falling."

What a fool! I believed them and with their help, got onto the seat. They steadied the bike, gave me a push, and I was off without either one of them on the sides of the bike. I quickly picked up speed as I wobbled from one side of the road to the other. An involuntary scream left my lips as I passed our house and hit the flat stretch of the road.

As I slowed down, it became harder for me to stay balanced. The huge oak tree across from the Jackson home was looming closer and closer as the bike seemed to steer itself in its direction. I went into the weeds, tipped to the side, and fell hard just before I would have crashed the bike and myself into the tree.

I slowly got up with tears in my eyes and examined my bloody elbow where it had hit some stones.

By the time Davey and Pete came up to me, I had stopped the tears and tried to act like a man. They both thought I did a great job for my first lesson and offered to give me another one tomorrow.

"No thanks. I think I'll wait until Dad gets me a bike."

"Suit yourself," said Davey as he and Pete got on their bikes and pedaled back up the hill towards Stump Road.

I watched them and saw them turn to each other more than once with big smiles on their faces.

A few months later Dad took me to a farm on Depot Road. An old man, Mr. Springler, took us out back to his barn where he dragged out a well-used bike that was just the right size for me. The tires were flat and it had some rust, but I thought it was grand.

Dad paid the man a dollar and loaded the bike into the trunk of our old, black Chevy sedan.

Mom helped me clean up the bike after Dad put air in the tires, oil on the chain, and adjusted the coaster brake.

It didn't take me long at all to find my balance with either Mom or Dad running along side of me. I was soon cruising up and down our street like nobody's business.

Heck, any bike riding seemed easy after Davy and Pete's riding lesson. I sure had some good friends!

THE QUARRY DUMP

I was around seven when Dad thought I was big enough to assign me the chore of taking the cans, bottles, and other junk to the old quarry across the field behind our house. All the neighbors who had property bordering the quarry threw their garbage into the quarry too.

Many of the stone blocks used to build Welch Allyn and the other factories in Skaneateles Falls were cut from the huge chunks of stone taken from it. Being civic minded, we were all doing our best to refill the great hole.

Most of the steep sides had been filled with junk over many years, but there were a few spots where it dropped down a good twenty feet. Dad warned me not to go near them and not to fall where all the junk was dumped because I'd surely get cut to pieces on all the broken glass and rusted metal and end up at Doc Horn's for stitches and a shot.

I had to drag the old potato sack filled with junk up the field. When I got fairly close, I pulled the sack as quietly as possible so that I might see some critters. The critters that the quarry housed were mostly giant rats. I always armed myself with a stone just in case I could get a shot at one and for protection.

As soon as the rats saw me, they took off in all directions burrowing into the maze of junk. Once I almost got one, but he jumped out of the way right before the stone hit the spot where he was sitting. They sure are quick, nasty creatures.

The rats gave me an uneasy feeling causing me to always look back over my shoulder when I left the quarry to make sure none of them were after me.

To add more excitement to the venture, I had to deal with Pal, the almost fire breathing pony. I approached the fence with caution and looked carefully to see if he was grazing in our field or out of sight in the woods behind the quarry.

If he was in our field, I put off doing dump duty until the coast was clear. There was no way I was going to try to cross the field with him nearby and ready to take a chunk out of my hide. I never felt completely safe crossing the field. I kept my eyes and ears at full alert for any sign of the charging monster while making sure not to rattle any of the cans and bottles in the dump bag.

PAINT JOB

When Mom got a notion to do something, it had to be finished yesterday. It's a wonder that all the housework didn't drive her to distraction because it was always there to be done again and again. I've never seen a woman work as quickly and as efficiently as Mom. Her hands danced and her foot and body positions were honed to perfection. No movement was wasted when she could concentrate on what she was doing. Heaven help my little brothers and sisters if they got "under foot" in the kitchen when she was in one of her frequent "no nonsense" moods. They, and I, quickly learned to stay out of her way when she got a certain narrow look in her eyes that seemed to focus only on the task that needed to be immediately accomplished.

One evening at supper time all of us, except Mom, were seated at the table in the small kitchen. I think there were four of us kids and Grandma Simpson in the house. After Dad called the blessing and Mom had served out the usual pile of spuds with a dab of some cheap meat, she asked for quiet.

She looked at Dad and said, "Vinnie, the old Chevy needs a paint job. It's got some rust spots and the black paint is looking very dull."

By this time Dad already had both sides of his mouth full of potato, and he looked like a huge chipmunk. He stopped in the middle of a chew and looked at Mom.

"Ethel, you know we can't afford to fix up the car. Why, we barely have enough money coming in to keep us under a roof and food on the table."

"I know money is tight, so I've been saving my 'mad money' for something special. I decided I can paint the car. I have enough put aside for a can of enamel paint, primer, sand-paper and a camel hair brush."

Dad said in a voice that already showed signs of defeat, "Are you sure that you can do it so it doesn't look worse than it already does?"

Mom looked toward the old ice box and said with a hint of indignation, "Didn't you tell me that I did a fine job of sanding down and painting it?"

Dad was getting trapped and knew it. "All right. When do you want me to get the paint and brush?"

"Thank you. Today is Thursday, so if you pick up the supplies on your way home from work tomorrow, I'll be able to get the job done on Saturday."

I forgot about the paint job until Saturday morning came around. Terry, Pat, and I were just getting ourselves situated in our normal spots in the living room to listen to the Saturday morning kids' shows on the radio. It was a few minutes before nine when Mom came in carrying our baby brother, John.

"Terry, you will have to be in charge of John."

Terry didn't look at all happy, but knew better than to protest.

I thought I was off the hook again and had escaped taking care of the baby until Mom suddenly turned to me and said, "Michael, get on your rubber boots and come outside with me."

Like Terry, I didn't dare protest because it always resulted in at least a tongue lashing and time in the bedroom. I got up quickly, went to the back entrance room, and got my boots on.

Mom poked her head around the corner and told me what she wanted me to do then finished whatever she was working on in the kitchen. When she came out, I followed her to the driveway pulling the hose and holding onto a bucket that had laundry detergent and water already in it.

I looked around to see where Dad was, but couldn't locate him. He must have gone up to his parents' house to check on them and get himself away from a possible future disaster site.

Mom gave me specific instructions, which mainly dealt with rinsing the car with great care after she washed it.

"I don't want to see a spot of dirt anywhere on this car when we are done. It has to be perfectly clean before I start painting it. And don't you dare spray me with the hose."

It took at least an hour for us to thoroughly wash the car and dry it off with old towels.

"Good job, Michael," she said as she stepped back to admire our work. "Now I have to sand off the rust around the wheel wells."

She grabbed some sandpaper and bent over to begin. Her hand was going around in a blur causing her butt to go back and forth with the motion. I thought it looked funny and started to giggle.

She stopped, stood up, turned around, and said, "What are you giggling about?"

I lied and said, "Nothing, Mom."

"Here. Take a piece of sandpaper and help me. Just do it the way I am."

She turned around and continued the sanding with me going at the rust on another wheel well.

As I sanded, I couldn't help but think of the **Buster Brown Show** I'd already missed and wondered if I'd hear any of the other Saturday shows.

"There. That ought to do it," she said as she wiped the final bit of paint and rust dust off the car with a clean cloth.

She opened a can of paint primer and primed the bare metal.

It didn't take long for her to finish.

As she cleaned up the camel hair brush in a small can of gasoline, she said, "Now we'll let it dry for an hour or two. You may go back into the house. Don't go wandering off beyond shouting distance because I will call you if I need some help."

After saying a quick 'thank you', I hustled back into the living room to catch the last of the kids' shows.

Shortly afterwards, Mom came in and started fixing lunch for us.

When we had finished eating, Terry washed the dishes. I dried them while Mom changed John's diaper and put him upstairs for his required afternoon nap.

The lack of noise from up the road told me there was nothing going on around the neighborhood, so I followed Mom outside to watch her paint the car. She quickly stirred the paint, poured some of it into a smaller container, pulled out the camel hair brush from her old apron, and began to paint. She first stood on an old chair so she could reach the top. Her paint strokes were fast and smooth and she always finished off an area with very light strokes to smooth out any brush marks. She only slowed down to use the edge of the brush next to the chrome. I watched carefully to see if she got any on the chrome and told her when she did. She quickly took a rag dampened in gasoline and cleaned off the offending paint before it had a chance to dry.

Once she was down from the chair and on the ground, her painting speed picked up even more. Every half hour or so, she stopped long enough to pull out a cigarette and have a smoke. She always stepped back and checked out her work to make sure it was done properly while taking deep pulls on the cigarette.

She had the whole car painted in about three hours. It looked really good!

"Now we have to pray that a breeze doesn't pick up and blow dust on the paint." She said this while looking up at the leaves in the nearby tree to detect any movement. Satisfied that there wasn't anything to ruin the drying paint, she poured back the extra paint into the big can, and washed her brush out in the tin filled with gasoline. As we walked back to the house, she turned around to admire her paint job. She looked down at me and smiled in a very satisfied way. I smiled back up at her.

Mom quickly got herself back into her "house" routine. After she got John up and changed and fed him, she started preparing supper.

Dad showed up just before it was time to sit down and eat. (He had a wonderful knack of knowing just the right time to reappear.) He already looked at the car and was so surprised at the job Mom had done that he set the table for her as a sign he liked her work.

After supper was done and the kitchen cleaned up, we all went outside to take a good look at the car.

Dad said, "Ethel, you did a fine job considering what you had to work with."

"Thank you. Now we can go on Sunday visits feeling better that we are riding in a car that looks almost new."

Mom was the next best thing to getting a job done yesterday.

MR. HANVILLE'S GREAT RIDES

Every school morning Mom got me up in time to get my hands and face washed and my wild, red hair combed. I could never get the cowlick to stay down no matter how much water I put on it.

I wore the same, worn dungarees for the whole week and changed my frayed shirts two or three times during the same time period, depending how dirty they looked. Many of my clothes were the ones Davy Walton had outgrown.

After getting dressed, I went into the kitchen and either had a slice or two of well-done toast or a bowl of cereal. Mom hurried me along with my eating and handed me the paper bag containing a peanut butter and jelly sandwich, two cents for milk, and a homemade cookie. Rarely did I get a nickel to buy an ice cream.

Double checking to make sure I was armed for the day, Mom gave me a kiss, told me she loved me, and to behave in school. (Behaving in school was always a problem for me, so I'd sidestep what she said by just saying, "I love you too," as I hustled out of the house and headed up to the corner to wait for the bus.)

Four or maybe five of the Waltons, two Kulle boys, Pete, Jimmy, and Nona Cashin, and I waited for the bus. We were all too tired to say much or fool around, so most of the time we just stood there like zombies.

We could hear the bus stopping and starting on County Line Road as the O'Hara boys, the two Walters, and Donny Kemblowski got on.

Many days Mr. Hanville, the bus driver, came to a speeding, squeaky halt, opened the door and said, "Hurry up kids, we're behind schedule again."

Mr. Hanville was a big, pleasant man with thick glasses perched halfway down his ample nose. His balding head was almost always covered by a broad-brimmed hat cocked to one side. He constantly wore a mechanic's shirt and pants. A big wad of gum was always in his mouth, which he worked with a vengeance in a vain attempt to replace a Camel cigarette.

Mr. Hanville often complained to all of us about having to drive the oldest bus in the Elbridge School District.

He probably got the rickety, problem ones because he was able to fix them if they broke down while making a bus run.

The kid who was last in line to get onto the bus had to worry about being closed in the folding door. I was often last because the older boys let the girls get on first. I was also too timid and small to push ahead of the other boys.

Without waiting for us to be seated, Mr. Hanville jammed the shifter into first gear and popped the clutch so it would engage the unhealthy transmission. If I had to find a spot toward the rear of the bus, I quickly grabbed the back of a seat to keep from falling as it lurched forward in loud protest, leaving a cloud of blue smoke in its wake.

We crossed over the creek, make a rolling stop at the Jordan Road stop sign, and started climbing the hill by Rodak's Bar. Mr. Hanville had to stop before he got to the top of the steep hill to load on the Miles' kids. We always ended up rolling back a few feet before the bus overcame gravity and slowly groaned forward up the hill.

By the time we made it to Vinegar Hill Road, the bus would be full of now suddenly quiet kids. We all got that way because we were anticipating the ride down the long hill a mile or so before Elbridge.

The big question that entered many of our minds was, "Will Mr. Hanville do it today?"

The bus had something called a governor that was supposed to keep it from going over 50. The machine was round and had a paper disk in it. The faster the bus went, the faster the paper went around. It was near the side window next to Mr. Hanville's left arm.

If the engine began to scream in loud protest as we approached the top of Vinegar Hill, we knew the answer to our silent question because the engine reached the governor controlled speed limit.

After cresting the hill, the bus sounded like a plane engine as we began to hurl down it. The trees close to the road flashed by in a long, giant blur, and the many loose nuts and bolts holding the bus together rattled almost as much as we did.

All of us started breathing again as the bus made it around the bend and hit the flats.

Mr. Hanville seemed to relax his grip on the big steering wheel, and I always noticed a twinkle in his eyes reflecting back at us from the rearview mirror.

The highest speed ever witnessed by a kid sitting in the front seat right behind Mr. Hanville was 72 mph.

We had about twenty seconds to get over that part of the ride and prepare ourselves for crossing the raised Auburn Railroad tracks. We all grabbed onto the back of the seats in front of us and braced. Mr. Hanville knew that the train never went through at this time in the morning and didn't bother with making an unnecessary stop before the tracks.

Once Bobby Miles forgot to hold onto the top of the seat in front of him as we crossed over them and almost hit his head on the ceiling. He came down hard with his lower jaw hitting the back of the seat. From then on, he made sure to secure himself.

It was a great relief to get off the bus in one piece. The ride was wonderful and nobody ever told on Mr. Hanville.

It's a miracle that a picture of a wrecked school bus with kids lying all over the road and in the grass was never published in the <u>Syracuse Post Standard</u>.

SCHOOL LUNCH

Lunch was one of my favorite times of the school day. My best times in school were spent on the playground. Lunch came in a very close second.

The lunch room was in the school basement next to the wood and metal shop classroom and across the hall from the boiler room. There were small slits for windows on an outside wall of the eating area.

If the Russians were going to drop a bomb in the area, lunch would be good a good time for them to do it because the whole basement hallway was our assigned bomb shelter Maybe we would be allowed to finish our last meal before we had to go kneel by the hall walls with our hands over the backs of our necks.

At our appointed lunch time, my class lined up in the hall outside of our room with either our bagged lunches or lunch money in hand and walked down the steel stairs.

Only the rich kids could afford to buy their lunches. After all, it cost twenty-five cents. The only time I got money for a school lunch was on the last school day before Thanksgiving. It was a real treat to have it then. Mom said that it was the only lunch during the school year worth twenty-five cents.

Those of us who just wanted milk got in the milk line and handed our two cents to the nice lady behind the cooler. The milk came in half-pint glass bottles from Mr. Hudson's dairy.

I sat down with some friends and prepared for lunch. First I took my sandwich and cookie out of the paper bag. Next, I carefully folded the bag and put it into my back pocket because

Mom said the bag had to last at least a week. After that, I un-wrapped the sandwich and cookie from the waxed paper, took the cardboard top off the milk, and ate.

We only had fifteen minutes to finish, so most of us wolfed down our food and spent the rest of the time talking.

The only time the lunch routine got interrupted was when a kid tripped and spilled his tray of food on the floor. We never tried to show concern but burst out laughing as a lunch lady re-trieved a mop from the corner and handed it to the unfortunate one who had the accident.

After lunch we were allowed to run around on the play-ground for a few minutes to help our stomachs settle and to burn off some extra energy.

It was hard to go back to class after lunch time. I always felt like napping and struggled to keep my eyes open once the teacher settled us down and started a lesson.

FIRST HAIRCUT

On a very warm summer evening we relocated ourselves to the front porch to escape the heat stored up in the house. Grandma Simpson wasn't with us because she liked to spend much of her time in her little bedroom reading books, writing in her diary, and avoiding the racket generated by kids ramming around the house.

Dad had run an extension cord from the living room socket and out the door so we could listen to the radio while we were cooled by the gentle summer breeze.

An ad came on the radio, and for no reason Dad started to chuckle.

Mom stopped rocking her chair and said, "What's that all about?"

Dad just smiled and seemed to be looking at nothing across the street.

"Well! The cat got your tongue?" Mom was getting very curious and so were we.

"I was just remembering Michael's first haircut by a real barber."

Mom worked up a slight grin and said, "I'd forgotten all about it. It sure must have been a sight."

Terry, Pat, and I were biting our tongues, but Terry could never bite hard enough on hers to hold it still.

"Please, Dad, tell us about it," Terry said with a little whine thrown in for added effect.

"Okay, but I first have to explain what circumcision means."

When he was done both girls had disgusted looks on their faces and Pat said, "That's an awful thing to do to a little boy!"

Neither Mom nor Dad came back with a reply.

"Anyway, Michael was around three and your mom and I decided that he needed a decent haircut from a regular barber," Dad said and then continued, "Keep in mind Michael wasn't circumcised until he was almost two.

"I walked him to Charlie Major's barber shop. As you know, Charlie also runs the post office. When we walked into the barbershop side of the building, Charlie walked through the door dividing the two businesses, said his hello to us, and put on his short, white barber's jacket. As soon as Michael saw him in the white jacket, he bolted out the front door screaming and made it to the front of the school before I caught up with him.

"I said to him, 'Michael, what's got into you? Mr. Major is only going to cut your hair. Settle down and come back with me.

"Michael kept screaming. I had to carry him back to the shop and saw that he kept his hand over his private parts.

"Poor Mr. Major really earned his twenty-five cents for that haircut. I've never seen a child carry on like Michael when getting a trim.

"After I paid Mr. Major and apologized for Michael's behavior, we walked back home. He kept a hand over his private parts until we were almost home.

"Mom came to the door when she heard him crying. She looked at him and asked what all the fuss was about.

"When I told her what had happened she stared at Michael. A look came upon her face as if a light went on inside her head. She said, 'Why, the poor child saw the white coat and thought he was going to be circumcised again.'"

Dad said, "Everything then became clear."

The girls had a good laugh at my expense.
John and I didn't think it was funny.

It's nice that most barbers no longer wear the short, white jackets.

PLUMS GONE WILD

Grandpa Quigley had a plum tree by the side of his house. It wasn't very big and its branches were low enough for me to reach. It was the first tree I ever climbed.

With a beet red face I strained to pull my bulk up onto the first branch. Once there, it was easy going to the last branch that could support my weight without bending too much in protest. I would be all of eight feet off the ground, which looked mighty far up to a boy of seven going on eight.

I liked to balance up there for a long time without moving, hoping for either Uncle Jimmy or Aunt Ann to come out of the house so I could scare whichever one came out. I didn't dare think about frightening either Grandpa or Aunt Mary because he might have a heart attack, and she probably would beat me almost to death.

Only once while perched in the plum tree did my wish come true. It was a Saturday morning. After balancing in the tree for a good five minutes and getting very impatient, I was just about ready to give up when the inner door to the back wash room opened and closed with a soft squeak.

It was Uncle Jimmy. I was surprised to see him up so early because I knew he liked to go out carousing on Friday nights with his friends and didn't get home until the chickens were about to get up for another busy day of pecking at the ground and laying eggs.

I tensed and tried to think of a scary thing to yell as my unknowing victim closed the outer door and shuffled towards the tree.

Jimmy was walking very slowly with his uncombed hair pointing every which way and his shirt tail sticking out of his pants.

I was getting excited as he approached the tree. Just as he got to within a few feet of me, I yelled, "Boo" as loudly as I could. (I know, "Boo" isn't very original, but I didn't have time to come up with anything better.)

Uncle Jimmy jumped a good foot into the air and let out a startled yelp.

"@#$% &!*+. What the %#** do you think you're doing?" Uncle Jimmy mumbled while holding the top of his head like he was trying to make sure it didn't come off.

The pained look on his face made me feel sorry I scared him, but I still had trouble trying to keep a straight face. I turned my head to the side a bit so he couldn't see me smiling and said, "Sorry, Uncle Jimmy."

"Don't you ever do that again or I'll redden your behind." He said as he moved to his car with unsteady steps, retrieving a pack of Lucky Strikes from the front seat, and weakly made his way back to the house.

I was very lucky that he was too much under the weather to come up into the tree and give me a good "what for."

I stayed in the tree for several minutes to make sure he wasn't standing just inside the back door waiting for me to come down. As I listened and watched, I happened to focus on something in the tree that caught my eye. It was round and turning from a green color to a purple one. I reached out and pulled it from the branch.

I never had a plum before and figured that the green and purple colors were standard. Mom said that they were good, so I wiped the plum on my pants to clean it and took a bite. It was a little hard and tasted just okay. While chewing around the pit and a worm hole, I saw that there were more of them. I stuffed four or five into my pocket and climbed down from the tree.

Once on the ground, I listened for any noise coming from the back room, decided that the coast was clear, and went behind Grandpa's barn to eat the stolen fruit.

When all of them were devoured, I came back around to the front of the barn. One of Uncle Jimmy's roosters was putting up a fuss. Slowly opening the barn door, I stuck my head through the narrow opening. I didn't dare to walk in without doing a safety check first, because if one of his roosters was loose, he'd probably attack me. The rooster making the terrible racket seemed to be okay. He was just taking out his anger on the metal top of his cage. After making sure the barn door was properly closed, I glanced towards the house and made sure the coast was clear.

Staying around Grandpa's house wasn't a good thing to do if Uncle Jimmy happened to see me back down on solid ground, so I decided to walk back home. Besides, it was getting close to nine and the kids' shows would be coming on.

When I entered our house, I made sure that the kitchen door didn't slam behind me. For some reason it drove Mom and Dad to a state of distraction if one of us came charging into the house and let the door fly shut.

Mom said, "Was anyone up at Grandma's?"

"Only Uncle Jimmy," I said as innocently as I could.

"What in the world was he up so early for?" Mom returned with a bit of surprise in her voice.

"He had to go out to his car to get some cigarettes." I said as casually as I could because I didn't want Mom to know what happened.

Soon after I got the words out of my mouth, my stomach began to growl very loudly and I didn't feel so great.

"Michael, was that your stomach? Didn't you have a bowl of cereal when you got up? Your color is off. I hope you're not coming down with something." Mom said all of this with no pauses and just a note of concern in her voice. She was used to one of us being sick with something at least a few times each month.

"I'm not hungry, Mom. I think I'll go into the living room and listen to the radio."

I half-heartedly said good mornings to Terry, Pat, and little Johnny as I entered the room.

Concentrating on the radio was a chore because my intestines were cramping up badly. The urge came on me quickly and I ran out the back door to the outhouse. I sat there hunched over in agony then felt a bit better.

When I came out, I saw Mom waiting for me at the back door.

"Are you okay, son?" She showed concern on her face and in the way she said the words.

"A little bit better," I said with pain.

"Michael, what have you been eating?" Now her voice had her detective tone.

I had to tell her what I had, how many, and what color they were.

"At least you're not going to die on us, but you will feel like it for a few more hours. Don't you ever eat unripe fruit again."

She was right. I had to make several more trips to the outhouse and it took a good two hours before I started to feel like I would live and could eat a bowl of cereal.

Uncle Jimmy didn't redden my bottom. The plums did it for him.

PICKUP GAMES

Enough kids lived in Stump City to field two teams with at least six of us on each side. Kickball, volleyball, and softball were the games we all liked to play the most. Usually the two oldest would pick teams. (I would feel good when I wasn't the last one chosen, which wasn't very often.)

Games were played at the Walton place because they had an almost flat backyard free of trees. We played so much that a dirt trail was worn through the grass between every base and on either side of the volleyball net. The bases were all made of scrap wood and the pitcher's mound was flat. The volleyball net was just a rope stretched between two poles.

The rules for each game were made in the distant past and almost set in stone. I say "almost" because something strange would happen in every game that didn't seem to fit any rule. The oldest kids would decide what was the right call and that was that. Nobody cheated, lengths of games were determined by the weather, light, and time for meals. When we finished, the champions of the day would celebrate, and the defeated would hope to be on a winning team the next time we got together.

I got all excited inside when I either kicked or hit the ball far enough to make it to first base. I wasn't the fastest or biggest kid in the area by any stretch of the imagination, and it was rare for me to get on base.

Somebody would always end up falling down or running into someone while going around the bases or fielding a ball, but tears of pain were rare and injuries serious enough to cause a kid to go home yelling for his mother were rarer still. The only time someone got badly hurt happened when we were playing baseball.

Dave Cotter lived in the main part of Skaneateles Falls on School Street and came over once in awhile to join in. He was a small, fast, fine baseball player. He'd often get a hit and steal a base or two during a game. One time he was on second and tried to steal third. He tried to do a professional type of slide into the base and caught his leg wrong on some rock or clump of dirt. We all heard a loud sickening, snapping sound and Dave began to scream.

Mr. Walton came running out of the house to see what the fuss was about. He checked Dave over and told him not to move. He ordered one of his kids into the house to call Dave's mom. It wasn't but a few minutes later that his mom was on the scene. Dave was carefully loaded into his mom's car and taken to the hospital in Auburn.

The next time I saw Dave, he had a cast from his hip to below his knee and was on crutches. He was in the cast for a long time and still walked with a slight limp when the cast came off. To add insult to his injury, he couldn't go swimming during the long, hot summer.

After the accident, Mr. Walton banned sliding into any base. Most of us thought it was an excellent new rule.

We continued to play games, and it didn't take long for the memory of Dave's painful yells to dim in our minds. We were soon going at it full tilt—minus the sliding.

FIELD DAYS AT THE AMERICAN LEGION

Late in every July the Valentine Meyer American Legion Post in Skaneateles Falls held its field days. The legion had taken over the Skaneateles Falls School once all the kids in the area started to go to Skaneateles for their education.

In the building there was now a bar in one of the former classrooms where the local veterans spent a lot of their free time over beer and whiskey talking about the two World Wars and the Korean Conflict. I wonder how long it took the men to get over the fact that they were drinking in a room which most of them probably used as a classroom at one time or another with a teacher standing where the bar was now located.

The hall walls still had pictures of students and teachers who had passed through. I found school pictures of all my aunts, uncle, and Dad. I noticed that I looked like Dad did when he was my age.

Anyway, several tents were set up at the backside of the building to shelter the gaming tables, and a big food tent was located at the far end by the back entrance to the school gym.

The older kids played the games while we younger ones watched as most of them lost their money.

My favorite game to watch had a table covered in green felt with different coins scattered all over it. There was always a silver dollar right in the middle. For a dime a player would get three metal rings. If he completely encircled a coin, the dealer would reach into his apron and give him the same amount as the coin he had rung. The toughest one to ring was the silver dollar because a ring was just big enough to fit around it. Many of the older kids lost more than their weekly allowances trying to do it.

The year I became old enough to play the games, I saved up thirty cents from my meager weekly allowance so I could try my luck at ring tossing.

As soon as it was time to open the gaming area, I went directly to the table and bought three rings from the table manager. I missed badly on my first two tosses and got a quarter on my third try! I got three more rings and let them fly. After almost ringing money on my next two tosses, I let the third one fly. The ring hit the table, rolled around in a circle and settled right over the silver dollar. I was in complete shock. I took my winnings and left the table. I was hungry and wanted to try some food and drink that I rarely got to eat at home and was eager to use some of my winnings on them.

I sure had a case of beginner's luck because I never broke even in the years I played the game after that day. In the long haul, the Legion ended up making money on me.

PONCHO VERSES THE LEGION AUCTION

One of the big highlights of the American Legion Field Days was the auction. The Legion members spent at least a month going around the community collecting donations of unneeded household items.

I went to my first Legion auction not knowing what to expect and wondering how things were sold. I got there early and stood to one side so I could see better and busied myself by looking around at the people in the crowd while we all waited for the auction to begin. I knew many in the crowd. Even Poncho was there.

Poncho was a short, middle-aged man. He wore old clothes, and never acted like a normal grownup. He spoke with most of the words coming out of his nose, making it hard for me or anyone else to understand him. To add to his speech problem, the left side of his jaw drooped down at a steep angle as if he put a pound of fishing sinkers into that side of his mouth just as soon as he got up in the morning. The slanted opening allowed his spit to run down onto his shirt like water coming out of a dripping faucet.

Poncho made his living by working at Waterbury Felt Company and mowing lawns. He never walked around the Falls in the good weather. Instead, he drove his lawnmower. It was a beat up thing with a muffler that only half muffled. The machine had a sound of its own. On a calm day I could hear him riding around on it from just about anyplace in the Falls.

Poncho loved his mower and kept it cleaner than he kept himself. The few remaining areas on the machine that didn't have rust were always shiny because he'd speed on home to clean his mower right after every cutting job.

Home for Poncho was a room in a trailer on School Street owned by Sam Cotter who had been kind enough to free Poncho from some institution.

I never knew nor did I ever ask anyone about which institution Poncho came from. Heck, I didn't even know his last name. I don't think he came from Mexico because he didn't have the same skin color or looks of the Mexicans I had seen in one of Uncle Danny's **National Geographic Magazines**.

Since he was standing close to me, I made polite and said, "Hello, Poncho, how are you today?"

He said, "Ho kay, I ggessh."

Greetings exchanged, I looked back to the front just in time to see three of the Legionnaires coming out of the side door of the old school. One of them was carrying a bullhorn, another a clipboard with a piece of paper on it, and the third a very old wooden chair.

The crowd slowly began to notice their arrival and started to simmer down. People who intended to stay for a long time planted themselves in chairs at the front.

The man with the bullhorn said, "Welcome to the Legion's annual auction. We have been fortunate this year to get many good items. I'd like to thank all of you who donated. For those of you new to the way we run our auction, let me explain the rules. If you raise your hand or nod in my direction, it means you have bid on an item. Once I say "sold", you will come up to the table and pay Bucky, pick up what you bought, and put it someplace out of the way. Any items left here past four o'clock will be put back inside where price tags will be placed on them. If they are still here in the morning, we will take them to the town dump."

The big things that stuck in my mind were raising a hand or giving a nod. I put my hands in my pockets and made my neck as stiff as possible.

The auction began with the old wooden chair. The bidding started at a quarter and quickly jumped to a dollar after a person in the crowd mentioned something about it being a Mottville chair. It sold for almost two dollars. This amazed me because the bottom was falling out and it was all scratched up.

It was fun to watch the people as they bid on things that truly belonged in one of the local dumps. Many items went for a nickel or a dime.

It was a good hour into the auction. Getting itchy, I began to loosen my neck a bit and took my hands out of my pockets. I forgot where I was and waved to Davey Walton who was standing on the other side. I immediately realized what I had done and quickly turned to see if the man with the bullhorn had seen me. He hadn't—probably because I was too short to see. I put my hands right back into my pockets and stiffened up my neck.

Poncho was still standing by me and hadn't said a word. He was completely focused on the auction but hadn't bid on anything.

A loud noise suddenly came from up front. It was the sound of an engine. I leaned to one side so I could see better. It was a freshly painted, gas-powered reel mower. At first glance it looked new, but when I looked closer I could see paint drips on the rubber wheels and on other parts where I knew paint shouldn't be.

Poncho came to life at the sound of the engine. He began to dance from one foot to the other and saying things in his strange, nasal voice. The spit began coming out of his mouth at a very fast rate.

The man with the bullhorn opened the bidding at fifty cents. A hand in the front went up just before Poncho's did.

This seemed to bother Poncho and he stuck his hand up even before the man with the bullhorn asked for a higher bid.

The man with the bullhorn said, "Do I hear two dollar?'"

Poncho's hand went flying up into the air again.

"Now, do I hear three?"

Now people were looking at Poncho when an amount was said. No one else was bidding except Poncho. Some people were smiling and trying not to laugh.

Even I knew Poncho was bidding against himself.

Before the man with the bullhorn said "sold," Poncho had bid five dollars on the mower.

Poncho quickly went up front and paid Bucky, the man at the table taking in the money, the five dollars. He left the auction with what looked like a big smile on his face as he trotted behind the mower heading toward home. He wasn't going to leave his prized possession there past four o'clock and have it taken away from him.

Before Poncho was off the Legion property and on his way up School Street, Sam Cotter, the man who owned the trailer where Poncho lived, went up front to have some words with the man with the bullhorn. I couldn't hear what was said, but the discussion looked serious and heated.

Right after he talked to the auctioneer, Sam went over to the table where Bucky was sitting with the cigar box filled with money placed in front of him. Bucky gave Sam some dollar bills. Sam left the auction and walked quickly down the road yelling to Poncho.

The tension that had been building in the crowd seemed to quickly evaporate and the auction continued. Most of the people in the crowd were decent and knew that the auction wouldn't be any fun if it went on with Poncho not getting some justice.

I learned some valuable lessons about auctions. More importantly, I learned about kindness and not taking advantage of people.

THE BOOB TUBE AFFECTS ME

I was about nine when we got our first television. The number of kids in the family was now five. Even Chris, the then youngest, would watch anything on television. Mom listened to the radio while she worked in the kitchen, but the rest of us didn't want much to do with it once we got the boob tube.

Shows that starred brawny frontier men really held my attention. I liked how they cleared the land, fought off Indians, rescued their women folk, and killed cattle thieves.

I got the idea that it would be fun to chop down trees from watching those shows. Knowing Dad kept an old hickory handled axe in the shed out back, got me itching to see if I could swing it like one of my heroes on television.

I came up with a plan and asked Mom if I was old enough to go into the woods between our house and Welch Allyn.

"Well, you are old enough, but are you smart enough to stay out of the filthy creek and not drown?" She had stopped her almost continuous work to say this, so I knew she was dead serious.

I put a thoughtful look on my face and rubbed my chin like Dad did when he was in deep thought about what he was about to say.

"I won't go in the water, and I won't go near any steep banks." I said this very slowly and tried to sound convincing.

"Okay. If you ever come back with cuts or wet clothes, your days in the woods will be numbered." This was said while she waved her finger at me in her most serious fashion.

I nodded my head and didn't say anything because I was really surprised she was going to let me go all by myself into the woods. I didn't dare tell her that I wanted to cut down trees with Dad's axe. That would surely put an end to my adventure right then and there.

After I thanked her and basically told her how wonderful she was without going over the line, I was all set for a grand adventure.

"You be back here within five minutes after you hear me call you for supper. You hear?"

"Yes, Mom. I'll be home in time."

I went out the front door and headed in the direction of the woods so she wouldn't get suspicious. (Mom was smart and would ask me why I was going out the back door when the woods were in front of the house.)

I walked along the side of the house where Mom couldn't see me from a kitchen window, stuck my head around the corner by the back screen door to see if she was in the area, and went to the shed. I remembered to be careful while I worked the shed door because sometimes it would squeak loudly when it was opened. The axe was in a corner under some other tools. I quietly moved the hoe and shovel to get my hands on the axe. I put the tools back where they belonged, slowly closed the door, and retraced my steps to the front of the house.

I carried the axe in one hand right in front of me because if Mom looked out, I didn't want her to see it. It was heavy, and by the time I was in the woods and out of sight, my arm was aching.

I put enough distance between myself and the house so Mom wouldn't hear the sound of the axe hitting wood and started looking for my first victim. I found what looked like the perfect tree some ten feet from the edge of the creek. It was in a flat spot and not close to a bank. On this day the creek water had a red color to it. (The shade of the water varied from day to day depending on what color was being used at Waterbury Felt to dye the blankets.) It looked kind of pretty.

Getting down to business, I placed the axe in my hands the same way I saw Dad holding it while cutting up wood and took my first swing. It wasn't much of a swing, but when the axe head hit the tree I still felt the jarring all through my body. I didn't know that a maple tree could be so hard. After several more swings, I was getting the hang of it, and small chips of wood began to flake off the trunk.

I worked a good ten minutes without stopping. When I did, I rested on the axe handle like Dad did and examined the tree. It was about forty feet tall and a good ten inches across where I was doing my chopping. I had only gone into the trunk an inch or so and realized that it would take longer than I thought before I could yell "Timber!"

I went back to swinging the axe and took short breaks to catch my breath. My hands began to hurt. I stopped and looked at my palms. I was getting blisters on both of them. When I went back to chopping, it hurt even more. I decided to stop for the day because I was having trouble gripping the handle and didn't want the axe to go flying into the creek.

I took the same route to the shed I took earlier, put the axe back where I had found it, and walked back to the front door.

Mom was in the kitchen and said, "Did you enjoy your first trip into the woods?"

"Yes, it was lots of fun. Can I go back tomorrow?"

"As long as you are careful and stay away from the steep banks and the water."

"I will."

After I said this, I noticed Mom checking me over for wet pants and blood.

Feeling a little guilty about using the axe dampened my spirits a tad, but the joy of swinging one was more powerful than the guilt I had.

I took caution not to let anyone see the blisters on my hands while we ate and tried to use them as normally as I possibly could.

The next day I was at it again. It hurt like the dickens to grip the axe and take swings until my sore limbs and hands got limbered up.

It took several days before the tree started to lean ever so slightly towards the creek. Since I had been chopping on the same side as the lean, I now moved to the back side of the tree before I continued my work. It wasn't long before I started to hear cracking noises coming from the wood. I got all excited and chopped faster. The tree finally protested with several loud cracks and began to fall.

"Timber!" I yelled loudly as I scrambled away from the base of the tree.

The tree made a dull whooshing sound as it ever so quickly passed through the air. It landed with branches cracking, leaves flying, and purple water splashing. It made it all the way across the creek and its lower branches were holding it up out of the water.

I was amazed and felt a deep sense of accomplishment that the tree fell where I hoped it would.

It didn't take long before temptation began to take hold of me. I tried to fight off what was going through my head by remembering what Mom told me before I left to go into the woods not more than half an hour earlier: "Stay out of the filthy creek and don't drown". But what Mom said was losing the battle with what came to be sound reasoning: I wouldn't be going into water but over it. All I had to do was make sure that I didn't get my shoes or clothes wet.

Temptation won. I put the axe down and stood on the base of the tree. I slowly edged myself out a bit further and jumped up and down a few times to make sure that the tree had settled. Deciding that the tree wouldn't move or be pushed downstream by the strong current, I worked my way slowly from branch to branch. I made it across without any trouble and only had one minor slip that sent my heart clear up into my throat.

I didn't do any exploring on the other side of the bank because I was anxious to see if I could make it back in one piece.

I had no problems and over the next few days gained confidence and speed as I went back and forth.

This was something that I couldn't keep to myself, so I told Davey Walton what I had done. He came down to check it out and was amazed at what he saw.

Word quickly spread among the youngsters in the neighborhood, and the tree was used as a short cut to get from Stump City to the northern end of Skaneateles Falls.

Before I got tired of chopping down trees, I had four of them crossing the creek. My labors were rewarded because the kids all thought it was grand to have thrilling walks across them.

It's a miracle that not a single child drowned during that period of cutting down trees. It's even more amazing that none of the grownups found out about it. (At least, that's what I thought at the time.) Drowning would have been a pleasant way for me to go if Mom ever learned about what I had been up to.

DIRT CLODS AND ASBESTOS SHINGLES

Uncle Jimmy decided that he had painted his parents' house too many times and talked to Grandpa about putting shingles over the clapboard siding.

Grandpa told Jimmy that it was a good idea and would pay for the shingles and nails if Jimmy put up the shingles. Uncle Jimmy agreed.

After the color and style of the asbestos shingles were selected, Grandpa paid for them. They were delivered and stacked on pallets at the far end of the stone driveway close to the plum tree where they sat for a very long time.

Between working and going out with the boys on the weekend, Uncle Jimmy was hard pressed to find the time to get the job done. (Having a grand time was Uncle Jimmy's top priority—not shingling.)

I watched Mr. O'Hara plow the field right next to the driveway so he could plant hay for Pal and his cow, Betsey. Before he got back to disk and drag the field to smooth it out for planting the seed, it turned very dry and the dirt formed into clods of various sizes.

I had just finished a visit with Grandma and Grandpa and was gently closing the porch door when my eyes looked to the direction of the plowed field. Without giving it a thought, I walked into the field and picked up one of the clods and tossed it into the air. When it landed, it broke into lots of pieces and a cloud of dust came up from the ground. I was soon pretending that I was tossing grenades at evil army friends of Hitler and blowing them up. To make my new game more believable, I started making loud noises as the clods hit the ground and broke into pieces.

I was so busy destroying the enemy I didn't see Davey and Pete coming down the road next to the field.

Pete said, "What are you doing, Mike?"

When I told him, both boys thought it was a great idea.

It wasn't long before we were lobbing "grenades" at each other. We'd throw them high into the air and watch the others dodge instant destruction.

During a slight pause in the action, I picked up two handfuls of clods and ran behind the stacks of shingles to use as a bunker. I started throwing dirt imitating soldiers lobbing grenades in movies. It wasn't but a few seconds later before Davey and Pete were lobbing clods back at me. It was great fun for a long time, and we would have kept on playing except our stomachs were telling us it was getting close to lunch time.

After saying our departing "See yah's", we all took off for home. I didn't think anymore about it until a few days later.

I was sitting at the kitchen table reading the comics when I looked up to see Uncle Jimmy at our kitchen door looking very hot under the collar.

"Michael, get your %## out here." He said softly and with a hint of anger in his voice.

I didn't dare say anything as I walked onto the porch and stood in front of him.

"Why did you damage the shingles in the driveway? What's wrong with you?"

He still looked red around the gills. I didn't know what to say because I couldn't figure out how I damaged the shingles.

"I didn't do anything to the shingles, Uncle Jimmy."

"You're wrong about that. Many of the ends are chipped and many of them are covered with dirt."

In a flash I remembered the clods of dirt. I never thought about what the dirt could do to the shingles because we were having such great fun pretending.

"I'm sorry, Uncle Jimmy. I didn't know that I ruined them." I said this as sincerely as I possibly could.

Uncle Jimmy didn't say anything for a good long time. He just stood there looking at me causing me to shift from foot to foot in an attempt to calm my nerves.

For some unknown reason, a slight smile came across his face and he said, "I know, Michael. You didn't mean any harm. But don't you and your friends play around them again. You hear."

Yes, Uncle Jimmy. I guess I did something really dumb."

"Don't worry about it. Boys will be boys." He was rubbing the top of my red head while he said it.

All was right with the world again.

I really liked Uncle Jimmy before. Now I liked him even more.

SLEDDING MAKES AN IMPRESSION

Soon after the Christmas Santa Clause left me a brand new American Flyer sled, I started getting very itchy to really use it. There were too many bare spots to chance scratching up the metal runners, so I only made short runs on the few spots with snow. I was also anxious to see if the closed-looped back runners made the sled go faster than the straight, sharp ends on my old sled.

After the first really good snowfall of the season, the word quickly spread around the community that kids were gathering on Walton's hill to sled. I quickly got dressed, which involved putting on a hat, gloves, a well-worn winter jacket, and rubber boots, and hurried up the road pulling my new sled.

Many kids were already making runs. No one had made it to the bottom yet because the snow wasn't packed down enough. It didn't take long before we were making it all the way down the hill and onto the flat area. With each run we all went a bit faster.

Not long after we began making fast runs down the hill, a kid grabbed the back runner on someone's sled and pulled. This caused the victim to turn sharply and spin out. Soon we were all at it. Kids were tumbling off, and sleds were either tossed upside down or continued to the bottom without riders. The object of the game was to make someone spin out and continue to the bottom without being spun out by someone else.

Being one of the youngest, I didn't do too well. I might have been one for ten when we noticed Charlie Bergeron slowly hauling his massive body up the road by the hill. Charlie was late getting there because he lived down County Line Road and it took word longer to reach that neck of the woods.

Charlie was a real nice guy who was much taller and heavier than any other kid in the area. He weighed in at well over two hundred pounds and was a good head taller than most of us.

We all tried to spin him out, but couldn't. He always make it to the bottom with at least one victim left sprawled out somewhere in his wake.

All of us were having a great time and ignored our frozen pants, feet, and hands. I learned to look to either side when I was at the top and took off when I thought no one was looking. This method worked well, and I made it to the bottom on most tries without being spun out.

I must have been getting cocky or just didn't look carefully enough because I made it only halfway down when I suddenly got spun out by a blindsiding sledder.

I tumbled two or three times and looked up the hill for sleds heading in my direction. What I saw scared me. Charlie was less than ten feet away and gaining ground quickly. He tried to steer around me but couldn't. Before I had a chance to even roll over on my back, he was running right across my stomach. The pain was sharp and instant. It felt like I'd been cut into pieces. I rolled over in agony a few times and slowly got up whimpering.

One of the older boys, Bobby, saw what happened and came running down the hill.

"Mike, are you okay?" He seemed surprised that I survived being run over by Charlie.

"I think so." I said with a small hint of courage.

Bobby said, "Let me see."

I lifted up my jacket and shirt. To his and my amazement, there were two red welts across my stomach.

I slowly recovered by walking back up the hill and rubbing myself. Of course, most of the kids wanted to see the damage Charlie had done.

After the rest of the kids made another four or five runs, I was feeling good enough to go down again.

From then on I made sure Charlie was well down the hill before I took off. I didn't want to press my luck. I knew I was very fortunate to still be sledding and not in Auburn Hospital or, even worse, being laid out at O'Neill's Funeral Home in Skaneateles.

MANY ARE CALLED, BUT...

It took a few years for my brain to dull the memory of not confessing a major sin during my first confession. I used a twisted method of rationalization to achieve this goal, and became a good, practicing Catholic. I always went to church on Sunday (If I didn't, Mom would have sent me to the Here After before my appointment time was up.), I never ate meat on Fridays, and I had done the First Fridays enough times to guarantee a priest being at my side to hear my final confession just before I died.

I felt called to become an altar boy. Besides, Pete and Davey had been doing the job for at least a year, and I didn't want to be left out.

I told Mom and Dad about my calling and they both were overcome with joy.

Dad said, "Michael, I'm proud of you. Did you know that I was an altar boy for many years at St. Bridget's and at one time wanted to become a priest?

"Really, Dad?" I said with awe because I couldn't imagine Dad being a priest with five kids.

Dad said, "I'll talk to the priest this coming Sunday to see if he needs more altar boys."

After church the next Sunday, Dad told us to wait outside for him while he talked to the priest. We hadn't been standing in front of the church very long when Dad came out the front door.

Dad looked at me and said, "Indeed, your timing is very good, Michael. Altar boy classes are starting up in two weeks, and Father is very happy that you want to try. Father said that you will have to study hard to learn all the Latin responses and what you have to do during different parts of the Mass."

I'd forgotten how Davey and Pete had complained about the Latin. This might be tougher than I'd thought.

I was at the church a few minutes before nine when the appointed Saturday arrived. It didn't pay to keep a priest waiting.

I was shocked to see Reverend McMahon at the front of the church. He was the head priest in the area and noted by both young and old for his no-nonsense style. Even the adults gave him a wide berth and always treated him with the highest respect.

What had I gotten myself into?

I said my greetings to Father as if I was talking to St. Peter himself, and he responded with a slight nod without any words being attached.

After Jimmy Bishop and Bobby Kulle arrived, Father McMahon talked to us for a long time about the seriousness of our jobs and concluded by saying, "If any of you boys want to get up and leave, now is the time to do it."

He made it sound like we were volunteering for a very hazardous mission during a war.

None of us moved. I was too scared to, and I also didn't want to disappoint my parents. Both Jimmy and Bobby looked like they wanted to leave too but didn't.

Father handed a small book to each of us and we began to go over our Latin responses to what he was saying in Latin. It was hard to say the words the way they should be said. All three of us were concentrating so hard that beads of sweat were breaking out on our foreheads.

Father kept us for an hour and gave us our memory assignment for next week. He concluded by saying, "I don't want any of you boys to come back next Saturday without knowing the responses."

I never spent enough time in school on anything to really learn what I was studying, so this was a brand new experience for me. There was no way I was going back next Saturday without memorizing all the responses Father had assigned.

Dad is the one who came to my rescue. He had taken four years of Latin in school, and, to my great relief, still remembered most of what the priest and the altar boys said during the mass. By the time Saturday rolled around, I felt confident and went to altar boy class feeling that way.

All three of us pleased Father. Both Bobby and Jimmy were better students than I was, so they didn't have to spend as much time studying.

It took eight Saturdays to get through all the responses and learn where to stand and what to do during a mass. We were each assigned altar boy gowns that almost fit. We wrote our names on the tags after we had crossed out the names of boys who had used them before us.

Father mailed us a schedule telling us the Sundays we would serve and who would be on the altar with us. He assigned all three of us different masses and each of us would serve with an experienced altar boy.

This was a great relief for me.

For my first mass, I served with Pete Cashin. All I had to do was copy him. I got up and sat down when he did and said the proper responses at the appointed times.

Just before Holy Communion, Pete and I had to stand closer together. To my great surprise, I heard Pete mumbling Latin responses while I said them.

I didn't trip over my gown, bump into the priest, or forget my responses during my first service. After I got my altar boy gown off and helped Pete put away things, I met Mom, Dad, and the rest of the crew in the front of the church. They were so proud of me.

Later that Sunday I ran into Pete and said, "Why did you mumble the responses?"

Pete said, "I only half learned them because I found out a few weeks into my altar boy classes that if I sat in the middle of the group of boys, the priest didn't catch on that I hadn't memorized the Latin."

Pete was not only older than me—he sure was much wiser.

GRAPES OF WRATH

Another Halloween was quickly drawing closer. The dark, gray clouds were flowing off Lake Ontario and hinting at the snows to come. The mornings were brisk, the maple leaves were all kinds of brilliant colors, and it was cool enough most mornings for Mom to make sure we put on light jackets before heading for the school bus to take another ride with Mr. Hanville.

The older boys, especially Davey and Pete, were again talking about raiding Mr. Pinker's grape arbor. Mr. Pinker and his wife lived right next door to Aunt Pat and Uncle Danny's house.

Both Pinkers spoke with a strong, foreign accent. I think they might have come from one of the "Slavia" countries. They were nice, hardworking folks who had raised many kids in their tiny house. In fact, they were the grandparents of the Kulle boys who lived right next door to the Waltons and just a few doors down from their grandparents.

In the past I wasn't asked to join in on the annual raid to steal grapes because I was too small. This year Davey and Pete decided that I was old enough to come along, which really didn't please me all that much.

I didn't dare to say no to them because I didn't want to let on that I was scared. The stories I heard of past raids, which always involved Mr. Pinker charging out of his house with his dog leading the way, made me feel thankful that I hadn't been invited.

Pete and Davey took me on their scouting mission a few days before the planned raiding date. Just after dark we snuck across the road and went between Big Jim's and the Calnons' house and behind Uncle Danny's garage with all the china in it. There was a fence running all around the Pinker gardens, and it came real close to the garage. We figured that the best way over the fence would be to put the old ladder leaning against the back of Uncle Danny's garage on the fence and climb over.

That decided, we sat for awhile listening for any signs from Rusty, Mr. Pinker's very mean cocker spaniel. We all believed that the dog's sole purpose in life was protecting his master's property. Rusty was now getting on in years and just sat on the porch when I walked by. But, a few years earlier he'd come charging off the porch and down to the road with the fur on his back standing on end and his teeth bared. Once I got past the Pinker property line, the dog would come to a screeching halt, turn, and trot back to the porch to resume his guard duty.

The three of us sat quietly by the fence for a good ten minutes. We stayed there that long without moving because we wanted to see if Rusty was doing any patrolling in the grape arbor. We didn't hear anything and decided we'd meet on Friday night after supper in front of Pete's house just before it got too dark to see.

Mr. Pinker didn't treasure the grapes themselves. He was more interested in the potent by-product. It was rumored in the community that he made the best wine for miles around and kept a huge supply in his basement.

On Friday I started thinking about the raid before school finished for the day. A mixture of both fear and excitement were running through my head.

At supper, when the noise level at the table came down to a dull roar, I asked Mom if it would be okay for me to go up to Pete's house and stay until after it was dark.

She looked at me and said, "Just as long as you and Pete don't do any early Halloweening. One or two days a year is enough of that and Halloween is not until next week."

"We aren't going to do any window soaping, Mom." I said this like a lawyer carefully choosing his words before a judge.

"All right, then. Make sure you are home before eight."

It was getting pretty close to dark by the time I finished helping to clean up the kitchen. I then remembered that Davey had told me to wear dark clothes and a hat. I hustled upstairs and changed my clothes, ran out the back door, and crossed the field to Pete's house.

I was out of breath by the time I rounded the front of the house.

"Where have you been? It's almost too dark to see where we're going." Pete said this in an agitated, anxious tone.

I mumbled something about a late dinner and dishes while they half listened as they started running across the street with me right behind them.

We slowed down to a crawl to cut down our noise level once we reached the back of the Calnon house and approached the back of their garage. Davey carefully put the ladder against the fence while Pete and I listened for Rusty.

Davey was the first one to the top of the ladder and quietly jumped to the ground some five feet below. Pete followed Davey, and I went last. When I hit the ground, I landed on a rotten branch and it snapped. We all froze in complete fear and listened. Nothing.

I followed the boys to the nearest row of grapes and began stuffing my jacket pockets with them. In short order we were ready to make our get away.

When we got back to the fence, we all realized the flaw in our plan: How were we going to get back over the fence with the ladder on the other side?

Pete dropped the grapes in his hands and began to haul the ladder over the fence. One of the rungs got caught on something, so he gave the ladder a yank. He must have been leaning back too far because he went on his back with the ladder landing on top of him.

The racket awakened a sleeping dog, Rusty! He began to growl and bark in a savage way. Right after he started, a light came on in the Pinker kitchen.

My heart was in my throat as Davey put the ladder on the fence. Both Pete and Davey tried to climb up the thing at the same time. Pete's fear must have been much greater than Davey's because he was up the ladder and over the fence before Davey regained his footing.

I was right behind Davey. Rusty's growl and bark were much too close and foreign swear words were coming from Mr. Pinker as I heard the kitchen door slam behind him.

I don't remember climbing the ladder or dropping down onto the ground on the other side, but I do remember being on my hands and knees facing the fence. Rusty was inches away from my face. It was very dark, but I could see the yellow in his eyes and smell his foul breath.

I was up and running and passed both Davey and Pete before we got back to the front of Pete's house.

We were all out of breath, scared, and excited.

Pete signaled us to follow him to the back of his house. We stood there pulling smashed grapes out of our pockets. Then we sat down on the back stoop eating the evidence.

Halfway through the feast, Davey began to laugh. Pete and I joined in. The feeling of friendship among us grew in an instant. We were like soldiers in combat who had experienced the horror of war and lived to tell about it.

We parted without saying a word.

When I got home, I went upstairs and changed my clothes. I told myself to remember to help Mom with the Saturday washing so I could put the grape-stained pants into the washing machine when she wasn't looking. For the time being, I hid them under my bed.

When I got back downstairs Mom said, "What did you do with the boys?"

"Not much. We just stayed pretty close to Pete's house."

I didn't lie, but the truth was stretched a good quarter of a mile.

Mr. Pinker never said anything to any of the neighbors because I didn't hear anyone talking about grape thieves.

It's strange, but I've never had grapes that tasted so good before or after that night.

SLEDDING AT BEAVER MEADOW

The newness of my sled was worn off. By the end of the last winter I had stopped worrying about nicks, dents, and scratches.

Just after Halloween we got enough snow to get some early runs in on Walton's hill. I continued to stay out of Charlie's way and was now spinning out my share of kids, especially the younger ones. The Sheridan boys were good targets because they were younger and were now being baptized under fire just like I had been.

Someone mentioned that the O'Hara boys told him that they used to sled down a very steep, fast hill right by the edge of Beaver Meadow when they were younger. They even told him where it was.

The older boys talked it over and decided that the walk might be worth it, so we all followed them up Stump Road and across the field to Beaver Meadow.

The boy who had talked to Bob and Dick O'Hara was true to what he had said and led us to a monster hill.

The narrow path running down the very steep hill had many clumps of huge thorn bushes guarding its sides. Two hundred feet or so down the hill, another large clump of dangerous looking bushes was growing right in the middle of the opening.

I stood there taking it all in and decided that a skilled sled rider would have to go to the left or right of it and stop his run on short, flat areas digging his toes deeply into the snow and dirt to stop himself from running into a wall of bushes.

We all clumped together like a herd of sheep looking down at the ground, making small talk, and trying to act brave. No one seemed to be in a hurry to be the first to go down.

Without saying a word, Pete jumped onto his sled and took off down the hill. There was just enough snow to cover the dead grass and bare areas, so he quickly gained speed.

When he got close to the bushes in the middle, it looked like he was going to go straight into them. At the last possible second, he dug his right toe into the snow and dirt and turned quickly to the right. Just after, he dug both toes into the ground, and he stopped about twenty feet short of disaster.

We yelled down to him with praises and started whistling our admiration of his bravery.

Pete got off his sled, raised his hands over his head and put them together like a champion boxer. The only thing he didn't do was bow.

All of a sudden, we all got quiet. It was as if we all had the same thought at the same time: Whoever doesn't go down will be called a chicken for at least a week.

Davey was the next to launch himself as the rest of us watched. To show Pete up, he went to the left and did a great side slide to stop. When the cloud of snow cleared, Davey was standing up and waving for us to come down.

A few more boys got up enough nerve to go down, and then I sensed the others were waiting for me.

On a stupid impulse, I decided to do a running start to get extra speed. With the snow only inches away from my face, I was soon going faster than I'd ever gone before on a sled. A thought crossed my mind—Why did I use waxed paper on my runners this morning!

The Great Divide came quickly, and I reacted just fast enough to miss the major part of the deadly clump of thorn bushes. I did hear something rip just behind me as I dug my toes into the snow and down into the dirt.

When I got up, I was surprised that I was still in one piece. I noticed a draft and looked down to see a big rip in my pants just below the knee. Mom sure wouldn't be happy about that!

I was shaking with relief, took a deep breath, and thanked the Almighty for sparing me a horrible death.

The rest of the kids came down. Some chickened out and rolled their sleds not long after they started. One had bad luck and hit a half covered rock and bent a runner, and the last victim, Corky Sheridan, took a spill just before the divide and rolled into the bushes.

He was very lucky because his Mom had bundled him up in many layers of clothes. Only one thorn got through everything. He gave out a mighty yell when Davey pulled the thorn out. The way he yanked it out reminded me of a movie I saw where the good cowboy pulled an arrow out of a wounded friend just before he died.

The walk back up the steep hill tired us all out, so we used it as an excuse to avoid another run.

We left the hill feeling happy that we had lived and vowed to try it again when the real snows came. I think many of us hoped the snows wouldn't come too soon.

MILK BY THE GALLONS

Mr. Hudson was our milkman for as long as I could remember. The only time he didn't deliver it to the house was the year Dad had the Holstein milking cows at the Olmstead farm.

We were now going through a gallon of milk in no time. Mom and Grandma Simpson were the only ones who never touched the stuff.

To save some money, Dad and Mom decided to buy it from a local farm on County Line Road owned by Mr. Staples. The farm was a bit past the O'Hara place.

After the price was set at twenty-five cents a gallon, Dad bought a stainless steel gallon milk pail at the Agway store in Jordan.

I quickly found out how the milk was going to get from the farm to our house. Mom and Dad had secretly decided that I was big enough to carry the milk, so I got the job.

Going up to Stump Road and then down County Line Road was the long way to get to the Staples farm. Besides, I'd have to walk by the O'Hara house. Bullet, the O'Hara boys' dog with the disposition of a rabid badger, would surely chew me to pieces if he saw me passing his territory.

The simple solution to the problem was to take the short cut through the Kimak field at the end of our road. The field was overgrown with weeds because it hadn't been plowed in several years, but a narrow path had been worn down by people living near Stump City as a way to cut some time off getting to Skaneateles Falls. Marty, the town drunk, had started the trail to get to Rodak's Bar and was its main traveler. I say 'was' because he stopped taking it after his near-death experience with Mom a few years earlier.

The route decided, arrangements made with Mr. Staples, and the pail purchased, I was ready to start the job.

As Mom handed me a quarter she said, "When you get to the farm, go through the milk house door and into the barn and wait for Mr. Staples to have a free moment from milking. He will fill up the pail. Make sure to give him the quarter."

Mom made me repeat what I had to do and added, "Be very careful carrying the milk. I don't want you tripping and spilling the lot of it."

I promised that I would and left the house pail in hand.

By the time I got to the end of the road and started walking behind the Kimak house, I had to switch the pail from hand to hand several times. The stainless steel container was heavy when it was empty.

I hadn't walked more than fifty feet down the path through the field when a huge black snake came across no more than a few feet in front of me.

I nearly jumped out of my skin. I both hated and feared snakes. I quickened my pace and kept a sharp eye out for any more of the monsters.

When I got to the opening in the hedgerow at the edge of the field, I was right next to County Line Road. The Staples farm was just across the street.

I went straight to the milk house and opened the door. The milk cooler was on the left and a ten gallon stainless steel milk can was on the floor next to it. Its lid was off and a huge milk strainer with a filter was stuck in its open top.

After I placed our pail on top of the cooler, I opened the inner door and entered the main barn. Mr. Staples was squatting down by a cow and preparing it for milking. He had a bucket of water with something that smelled like iodine in it close by. He reached into the bucket and pulled out a cloth and gently cleaned each utter. When he was finished he threw the cloth into the bucket and put the milkers on each utter.

He must have known I was there because he didn't act at all surprised when he stood up and turned toward me.

"Hello, Michael. You must be here for some milk." He said this while walking past me toward the milk house.

I followed him as he said, "How's the family doing?"

"Everyone is just fine, thanks." I replied. To be sociable I added, " I hope Mrs. Staples and Roberta are okay."

"They are."

By this time we were in the milk house, and I was wondering how he was going to fill our milk pail.

My silent question was answered when he took the strainer off the top of the huge container and tilted it towards a five gallon bucket. He then put the big container upright and placed the strainer back on the top. This done, he picked up the bucket and poured the milk from it into our pail. He didn't spill a drop.

While he put the lid on our pail, I fished in my pocket for the quarter.

When he stood up I handed him the money and said, "Thank you, Mr. Staples."

He nodded, waved a good-bye, and went back to his milking.

I reached down and grabbed the handle of the milk pail and was surprised at how heavy it was. It almost weighed as much as half-filled buckets of coal I had to haul up from the cellar on a daily basis during the heating season.

By the time I reached the other side of the hedge row, my left arm felt like it was a foot longer than my right one and my shoulder was aching.

I didn't switch hands until then because if Roberta, the Staples girl, had seen me, she would have thought I was a weakling. Roberta was as tough as nails from all the work she had to do on the farm, and I wasn't going to let some girl think she was stronger than I was.

Between switching hands, looking for snakes, and staying away from any rocks that might cause me to fall, it seemed like it would take forever to get across the field.

Once I made it to the Kimak lawn, I felt relieved. Now all I had to do was get the pail of milk home before one of my arms fell off.

When I finally went through the kitchen door, my upper body was in agony.

Mom said, "That was quick. Was the pail too heavy for you?"

I stood up as straight as my sore shoulders would let me and said, "I managed okay."

"Good job. The way we go through milk, you'll be making the trip every two days."

"I can handle it, Mom." I said this with slight conviction because I felt pretty worn out at the time.

For several years I did make the trip almost every other day. The only time I got a break was when Dad decided he'd drive down to get it, which wasn't very often.

My brief talks with Mr. Staples fell into a routine that was almost the same as the first words we had spoken to each other. The only thing that changed was the size of the container. As we kids grew in size and number, the pail went to a two gallon size. By the time we stopped buying milk from Mr. Staples, I was carrying a two gallon pail in one hand and a gallon pail in the other.

A few times I took the long way there and past the O'Hara place when the snow was too deep to cross the field. When I got close to the O'Hara place, I walked as silently as I could down the stone road and prayed that Bullet was either behind the house or in the barn. He did try to attack me a few times, but I quickly found out that an empty or full milk pail is a good weapon and he stayed just out of range.

Seeing snakes in the field ended up being more in my head rather than on the ground in front of me. I never did see very many—just enough to keep my fear and imagination working overtime on each trip to the farm.

RAT SHOOT

I was in the front yard on a Saturday afternoon putting away my Marx electric train set. I came up with the idea of setting it up on the grass and running an extension cord from a plug inside the house to the transformer. I was smart enough to wait until all the dew had dried off because I didn't want to chance getting electrocuted when I turned on the switch.

My experiment didn't work that well because the grass was just long enough to come up around the tracks causing electric shorts in the track and some derailments. I even spent lots of time using Mom's hand shears cutting the grass, but that only helped a little bit.

I was putting the last piece of track back into the box when I heard a gun shot. It sounded like it was coming from up the road by the Walton house. Within seconds, I heard another round go off.

I quickly got my train set put away and ran up the road. Just as I got to the top of our street, a third shot went off. It was coming from the dump across the street from the Walton field. Someone was shooting the gun near one of the community dumps by the creek bank.

I took the path into the woods that led to the dump and eventually to the Waterbury Felt Company. I got close to the dumping spot and saw Davey and Pete standing by the edge. Pete had a bolt action Marlin .22 rifle and was taking aim at something.

Davey saw me and put a finger up to his lips to signal me to be quiet.

I slowly walked up to them. Pete still had the rifle in a firing position.

As I looked down into the dump to the area where he was aiming, I saw something move. It was a huge rat. A split second later I jumped when Pete fired the rifle. The rat also jumped and came down flopping around like a fish on dry land.

Davey said in a soft voice, "Nice shot. Now it's my turn."

Pete handed the rifle over to Davey. Davey worked the bolt to eject the empty shell and put a live round into the chamber.

"Whose gun is it?" I whispered into Pete's ear.

"It's my brother's," he whispered back.

Continuing in a quiet voice, I said, "Does he know you have it?"

"No. And you better not tell him." he said in a slightly threatening tone.

"I sure won't."

I thought of Jimmy, Pete's older brother. Jimmy made a nail look soft and surely would beat the daylights out of Pete if he ever found out he had his rifle.

Another rat came out and Davey blasted him. The rat didn't even twitch.

Davey gave the gun back to Pete.

We stood there being very still for a few minutes. The rats thought the coast was clear and started to come out. There must have been ten of them.

Pete took aim and fired.

"%*#+," I missed him. "Here, it's your turn."

I couldn't believe that he was speaking to me. He knew I hadn't shot anything bigger than Dick Kulle's B.B. gun.

Pete handed me the weapon, showed me how to reload it and said, "Keep it pointed towards the dump. We don't want any holes in us."

I nodded and lifted the rifle to my shoulder. It was much heavier than a B.B. gun. It didn't take long before the end of the barrel started waving back and forth. Just when I thought I couldn't hold it any longer, a rat popped up between two rusty cans. I pulled the trigger and the can in front of the rat went flying into the air.

Davey said, "You almost got him. Aim a little higher the next time because you're shooting down a hill."

Davy and Pete each took a shot and sent their victims to the Big Dump in the Sky.

It was my turn again. This time I was lucky. A dumb rat came out of his bunker no more than ten feet from me. I remembered to aim a bit high and got him.

Davey said, "Great shot!"

Pete looked down at his wrist watch and said, "Oh, oh. Jimmy will be back from Skaneateles in a few minutes. I've got to get home right now."

Pete grabbed the rifle from me and barreled on home leaving Davy and me behind without saying a departing word.

Davey looked back from Pete's high speed exit and down at me. "See ya," and gave me a wave as he took off for home.

I was left there thirsting for more rats and a gun to shoot them with. The crack of a rifle being fired and the smell of gun powder were what I was wanting. I knew that I was years too young to have a real gun and not quite old enough to have a B.B. gun.

It was a terrible feeling to be between having things because of being a certain age. I had gone through it once before when I wasn't at the right age to start riding a two wheeler and was still stuck on my tricycle.

I thought about this for a few minutes and decided that there would be more things coming along my way where I'd be too old for some things and not old enough for others.

GONE FISHING

Uncle Jimmy was finally putting the last pieces of siding on Grandpa's house. He was on a step ladder, and I handed shingles up to him one at a time when he called for another one.

Out of the blue he suddenly ceased his constant whistling and hammering. He stopped doing both only two other times when I was working with him—when he had missed nails and hit his thumb or finger. At those times I listened very carefully because I was sure to learn a new cuss word or two. Uncle Jimmy didn't disappoint me.

He looked down at me and said, "How would you like to go fishing with me next Saturday morning? The trout season opened a few weeks ago, and Hub Cashin told me his friend Pee Wee caught some real whoppers in Carpenter's Brook."

I felt embarrassed when I said, "Gee, Uncle Jimmy, I don't have a fishing pole."

"Not to worry," he said ignoring my reddened face.

He continued, "Ask your Mom if it's okay for you to get up early next Saturday morning to go fishing with me. Let me know what she says."

Uncle Jimmy knew that Mom was in charge of letting any of us kids do things, and she didn't bother bringing them up to Dad for his final approval.

"Okay. I'll come back up after we eat and let you know what she says."

"Good. Now hand me another shingle. The end of this job is in sight."

When we sat down to eat supper and Mom finished leading us in saying grace, I asked her about going fishing with Uncle Jimmy.

"It's fine with me, but you tell him he will have to answer to me if you drown or he takes you to some watering hole on the way home."

She knew both Uncle Jimmy and Dad loved to stop for a drink or two when they were out and about. She didn't want me in any place where The Drink was served. She couldn't control Dad taking me into a bar, but she knew Uncle Jimmy feared what she would do to him if he did something she had told him not to do.

After we 'Big uns' cleaned the supper dishes and kitchen in what Dad called an "All hands on deck" manner, I asked Mom if I could go tell Uncle Jimmy.

"Yes, you may, Michael, but you make sure to tell him what I said about taking you into a bar."

"Yes, Mom. I'll tell him."

I was out the back door and running across the field in a hurry and at Grandpa's house in no time. I made sure to knock and wait for someone, usually it was Aunt Ann, to say, "Come in".

It was Aunt Mary who invited me in. I was surprised to see her all dressed up like she was going to church.

The look on my face must have been telling because she said in a defensive tone, "What are you gawking at? Can't a lady get dressed up once in awhile?"

Grandpa was sitting at the kitchen table eating his dessert and Grandma was across the table in her wheelchair facing him. He had a smile on his face and a twinkle in his eyes. Grandma also had a twinkle in her eyes and what looked like a small smile on her face.

I fumbled out, "I'm sorry, Aunt Mary, but I thought you only got dressed in your Sunday best on Sundays."

She was about to lay into me when there was a knock on the front door. I heard Aunt Ann welcome someone in and noticed that Aunt Mary had now put a very angelic like look on her face. The only other times I'd seen her look like that were when she was talking to a priest or a nun.

As she walked out of the kitchen and into the dining room, I peeked around the corner to see what had made her change like she had just come back from Lourdes where I heard many miracles had been performed.

I saw a tall man with his hair well combed all decked out in his Sunday best.

Quickly I got my head back around the corner and walked to Grandpa Quigley who was waving for me to come over. When I got close to him, he made me lean close to him and said, "Michael, me boy, say a quick prayer for Patrick. He needs one badly."

I was looking across the table when he was saying this and saw Grandma nodding her head up and down.

I had no sooner stood back up when Aunt Mary came in with Patrick in tow. Aunt Ann was right behind him and almost invisible because of her small size.

"Mother, Father, this is Patrick, the man I was telling you about." Aunt Mary said this in a very formal, nervous voice with a big smile on her generously painted lips.

Patrick said some words to both of them about how nice it was to finally meet them and shook Grandpa's hand.

I noticed that Patrick seemed to be nervous too.

I almost died of shock when he said, "Mary is a fine young woman. You both should be proud."

Aunt Mary introduced me to Patrick and I was very careful to watch my manners and say the right things.

Aunt Mary said, "Well, we will be going now."

She turned to Aunt Ann and said, "Be sure to have Mom in bed at a decent time. She needs her sleep."

"Yes, Mary," was all that Aunt Ann said.

I noticed a hint of a command in Aunt Mary's voice but saw that Patrick was just standing there with a big grin on his face with his hands locked together in front of him.

After we heard the front door close, Grandpa sat there shaking his head and saying, "Love is blind. T'is surely blind, deaf, and dumb."

Aunt Ann began to laugh but suddenly stopped. She looked around the corner to make sure Aunt Mary hadn't come back into the house. Satisfied, she laughed some more.

Before I could use my reasoning on what had just happened, Uncle Jimmy exploded through the back door.

"I see that her highness has left. I had to stay out in the barn while Patrick was here. I was afraid I might open my mouth and give him a warning shot across the bow."

Grandpa and Aunt Ann began to laugh again. Grandma's stomach was going up and down and a sound almost like a laugh was coming from her mouth.

It suddenly dawned on me what they were laughing about, and I joined in.

When things calmed down, Uncle Jimmy turned to me and said, "Did your mom say it was okay to go fishing?"

"Yes, she did. But she told me to tell you that you weren't to take me into any bars."

Grandpa and Aunt Ann began to laugh again.

As their laughing died down, Uncle Jimmy said, "Fishing will not be complete without a drink at the end, but I'll do what your mom asks. Be up to the house by 5:30. I'll have the woody loaded and ready to go."

I said, "I will, Uncle Jimmy."

I said good-bye to everyone and headed on home. How was I going to get up before the sun?

I told Mom what had happened at Grandpa's house.

Mom said, "T'is true. Love is blind."

I would have added deaf and dumb, but it didn't make any sense to me why both Grandpa and Mom had said almost the same thing.

The problem of getting up so early was solved. Mom said that I could use their alarm clock. She would show me how to set it.

"You'll have to sleep downstairs on the couch on Friday night. I don't want the alarm waking up any of us. When you get up, you will set it for seven so your father can get up and be at O'Hara's Meat Market in time for work."

Before bed on Friday night, Mom made sure I had all the clothes out that I would need. She even placed my tall, rubber boots with the patched holes on the kitchen porch.

I jumped when the alarm clock started ringing and quickly turned it off. I then set it for seven and quietly went upstairs into Mom and Dad's room. I placed it on the night stand on Dad's side, pulled the blanket back over baby Chris who was sleeping soundly in the ever-present crib, and left the room.

Once downstairs, I quickly got dressed, had a bowl of corn-flakes, and gently closed the kitchen door on my way out. The boots went on easily because they were a good two sizes bigger than my feet. I think Mom had found them at the Thrift Store in the bottom of the Masonic Temple building in Skaneateles.

I hurried up the hill and across the field as quickly as the flopping boots would let me move.

Uncle Jimmy was leaning against the back door of the house smoking a cigarette.

"Ah, you're here on time. Let's go. The woody is all loaded up."

Without saying a word, I climbed into the front seat and got myself comfortable.

Uncle Jimmy took one last, long drag, flicked the cigarette butt into the field, and got in. He started the woody and gave it just enough gas to get it moving. He didn't want to wake up anyone, especially Grandma.

Once we climbed the steep hill by Rodak's and left the Falls area, he opened up the engine. It gave off a powerful roar, and we zoomed east to Route 321. Once on 321, he really put his foot down on the gas pedal. He steered around the sharp turns with skill, and we were at Carpenter's Brook next to the fish hatchery in no time at all.

He parked the car on the side of the road and we got out.

"Here. Take this rod and reel. We're in luck. No other fishermen are here. That will teach 'um to go out drinking the night before," he said with a sad laugh.

I laughed along with him because I knew how long he stayed in bed on Saturdays after he'd been out with the boys. This was truly a sacrifice on his part.

He reached back into the woody and got out his gear and a can of worms.

"Come on, Michael, follow me. We'll try fishing a bit in the big hole downstream."

We trudged along the muddy bank at a good clip. I noticed that the brook wasn't that wide and the water didn't look deep.

I was just beginning to get out of breath because of the pounds of mud I was hauling on the bottom of my boots when he suddenly stopped. He said, "We're here. Now, I want you to be as quiet as a mouse. We don't want to spook the fish."

He put his rod and reel down and showed me how to put a worm on a hook. He then cast the line out in the water for me.

"Hold the line between your thumb and finger like this. If you feel something pulling on the line, give the rod a yank up. You'll know if you got a fish on."

I expected to feel the line yank in a second or two, but I didn't. I watched Uncle Jimmy skillfully prepare his gear and cast his line in.

We stood there in silence. The muted sound of the quietly flowing water was occasionally interrupted by the sounds of birds coming to life and marking their territories. Once I heard something moving along the bank just downstream from us. I kept looking in the area where I heard the noise, but I didn't see anything.

"It's a muskrat, Michael," was all Uncle Jimmy said to me.

Just as I began to start daydreaming about giant fish, I felt a strong tug on my line. I yanked up just as Uncle Jimmy told me to and began to reel in the line. I was so excited that I started reeling backwards. I quickly realized my mistake and started doing it the right way.

"Keep the tip of the pole up. Don't let the line go slack," Uncle Jimmy was talking in a quiet, excited voice.

When I got the fish close to the bank, Uncle Jimmy leaned over and deftly got the fish out of the water.

"It's a nice brown trout. He must weigh a good two pounds."

We both examined the beautiful fish. Uncle Jimmy then grabbed the fish in a different way and put the palm of his free hand just below the fish's gills. He pushed back and the fish was dead.

After he put the fish in a sack, he bent over and rinsed off his hands in the stream. When he looked up, he smiled at me and gave me a wink.

"Great job, Michael. He'll taste good tonight."

It took him a good five minutes to unravel the knots in my reel. He had me hold his pole while he did it.

"Next time, don't get all excited on me and reel backwards."

"I'll try not to," was all I could say. Who knows what could happen in the heat of a big battle?

We fished for a couple of hours and caught five more fish between us. Uncle Jimmy told me to take the fish off the hook of the last one I caught, but didn't let me try to send him to the Promised Land. That's good, because I didn't know if I had the strength or stomach to break the fish's neck.

On the hike back to the woody, we talked about how great the fishing was and relived some of the better fights we had gone through. When we go to the road, Uncle Jimmy got down into the water to rinse off his boots and hands and had me do the same.

The fish and gear loaded into the back, we climbed into the woody.

The drive back home was much slower. When we got to the stop sign by Rodak's, Uncle Jimmy stopped his whistling and looked at the now open bar. I could tell he was fighting off a great temptation. He sighed and crossed the railroad tracks by Welch Allyn and took me home.

We both got out of the car. Uncle Jimmy had me go first carry the fish up to the house to show Mom and the gang.

They were all surprised to see the fine catch.

He asked Mom to get something to put the fish in and loaded three of them into the container.

"This ought to feed the herd tonight," he said.

"Why thank you Jimmy. I can't remember the last time I had trout." Mom said with delight.

He nodded and said, "Is it okay if Michael comes up tonight to eat with us?"

"That will be fine," Mom replied.

"Thank you, Uncle Jimmy. It sure was great fun. What time should I come up?"

"Supper should be ready around five," He said and added, "Maybe Aunt Mary will be staying home tonight and cook us a fine meal."

He and Mom both laughed.

I was so excited about the fishing that I wasn't at all tired after getting up so early. Heck, I didn't even mind that I missed the Saturday morning kids' shows.

I left our house a few minutes before five with the wonderful smell of frying fish filling my nostrils.

The same smell of frying fish at Grandpa's hit me before I got close to the back door. Aunt Mary was at the stove cooking the fish while Aunt Ann was running around the kitchen doing whatever Aunt Mary commanded her to do.

When it was ready, we all sat down to eat in the dining room. The fish was delicious.

Uncle Jimmy and I relived the morning for all to hear.

It was a grand time and a grand meal. Aunt Mary was even in rare, good humor.

When I left for home and was walking down Stump Road, a thought came into my head: Uncle Jimmy and I had caught some real nice fish. How had the fishing been for Aunt Mary?

BUGGY RIDE

The days of the horse-drawn buggy had been gone for some time by the middle fifties, but there were still plenty of them around. A buggy was nothing more than a small wagon used to carry a few people and some goods. Most of them were sitting in fields rotting slowing into the ground with broken wheels and bed boards. Some people still kept them in their carriage houses or barns either wishing for the return of horse transportation or just in case cars went out of style.

I was on my way to visit Grandma and Grandpa hoping Grandpa was well enough to tell me another tale about the Old Country. As I got close to the Cashin place, I could hear hammering and voices coming from the driveway side of their house.

Curious about the activity, I quickened my steps and soon discovered the reason for the noise. Pete and Davey were working on a beat up one-horse buggy.

"Hi, guys. What's going on?" I said.

Davey replied, "Not much. We're fixing up this old buggy."

I said, "Where did you find it?"

Pete answered, "Jimmy bought it for a dollar from Mr. Caddy."

"Oh." I said and added, "I'm going to visit Grandma and Grandpa for a bit. Can I come back and help when I'm done?"

Davey said, "Sure. We could use the help."

I remembered Mr. Caddy. He had retired from farming and sold out to Mr. Peters. He now owned a small piece of property next to his daughter's house on Irish Road. He and his wife stayed around the area until the snow began to fly and then drove to Florida to winter because the cold didn't agree at all with Mrs. Caddy. Dad worked for him as a boy and would now visit him once in awhile to catch up on Mrs. Caddy's health, the quality of this year's crops, and talk about old times on the huge Caddy dairy farm.

Grandpa wasn't up to telling me a story, so I stayed just long enough to pay my respects while I ate an oatmeal cookie Aunt Ann had just pulled out of the oven.

When I got back to the Cashin place, Davey and Pete were having a tough time trying to get the wagon tongs off. Wagon tongs are the two long, wooden pieces at the front of a horse-drawn wagon that the horse is attached to.

Pete said, "Mike, hold up the tongs while we loosen up the bolts."

I held them up while they cursed at the rusted metal. It took them a bit. By the time the tongs were off, sweat was dripping down their foreheads, cuss words were thrown at the rusted bolts, and my arms were beginning to ache.

I laid the tongs down on the grass next to the driveway and said, "What are you going to do next?"

Pete said, "Some of the buckboards are too weak to hold any weight, so we have to rip them up and put better boards down."

There was only one hammer, so Davey and I stood around trying to look helpful while Pete ripped the boards off.

After the last rotted board was pulled and thrown over by the tongs, Pete said, "Hand me one of the new boards."

Davey and I both bent over at the same time to get the board and almost banged heads.

"Here," Davey looked at the board and continued, "It doesn't look much better than the ones you just took off."

Pete replied, "Anything is better than the rotten ones I just ripped up."

He had a point, so Davey didn't come back with any argument. Safety and good wood weren't big issues when none of us had the money to buy new boards or parts.

Most of them had to be cut because they were too long. I held the boards on the saw horses while Davey did the sawing. He was good at it and only nicked a finger once. When he did, he responded with a few cuss words to show us that he was grown up.

When that part of the repairs was done, Pete said, "We'd better check the spokes. The wheels are awful wobbly."

Each of us found at least one cracked spoke in every wheel and began trying to think of a way to fix them.

We were all stumped until Davey said, "I've got it! I have all kinds of bailing twine in our barn. Maybe we can do something with it."

Pete and I agreed that it might be a way of repairing the spokes, so Davey trotted back to his house to get some twine from his barn.

While he was gone, Pete and I examined the buggy in silence. I decided that the wagon didn't look much better than it did when I saw it earlier. I remember Dad saying used car salesmen would "doll up" an old car to make it look better. In my view, the buggy wasn't "dolled up" very much at all.

Davey's voice interrupted my thoughts when he returned with an arm load of twine, and we were back at thinking of a way that the twine could help solve the problem. Pete decided that we could tie the bailing twine below the cracks in the spokes, tightly wrap the twine around and around the spokes, and finish off the job with knots.

His idea sounded good to all of us, so we got started. It took several tries before we figured out a good system, and the cracked spokes didn't move around as much as they did before we roped them.

Done, Davey climbed up onto the rickety seat. "Hey, how are we going to steer it?"

Without the tongs and horse in front of him and no reins to hold, he made a good point.

I looked down to the ground trying to pretend I was in deep thought. I noticed the leftover bailing twine and said, "How about using the twine? We could tie it to the front axle just inside the wheels."

Both of them looked like they were going into deep thought and didn't say a word.

I got the feeling they thought I'd come up with a good idea but didn't want to admit it too quickly. After all, I was a few years younger and shouldn't be beating them to the punch with good ideas.

I just stood there waiting for them to decide and was very pleased with myself when Pete said, "What do you think, Davey?"

He hesitated just long enough to give off a slight hint of doubt and said, "It just might work."

"Okay. Let's try it," Pete returned.

It didn't take but a few minutes and the job was done.

Now it was time to see how the buggy would handle with boy power. Since the buggy belonged to Pete's brother, Pete got himself up on the seat first while Davey and I pushed from the back.

The buggy was light and with its big wheels easy to push. We went real slow at first because Pete wasn't too confident about my steering idea. He experimented with different hand locations on the twine and found that if he let the twine run over the arm rests on either side of the seat, he had enough leverage to turn the wheels with some ease.

Davey was next to try. Pete showed him where to place the twine in his hands. Pete and I pushed Davy up and down the short driveway several times. My legs and shoulders were getting pretty weak when Davy turned around on the seat, looked at me and said, "Mike, give it a go."

He got down. I climbed up and grabbed the twine in the right spots and we were off.

The only other time I had steered anything this big was when Dad put me on his lap and let me steer the car. But, that didn't count because Dad also had his hands lightly resting on the steering wheel.

I hadn't gone up and down the driveway but a few times when I heard Mom calling me to come home for lunch. I was quickly learning that Mom's timing didn't match mine.

I told the guys I'd be back soon and hurried on home.

During lunch I told everyone at the table about the buggy and what we had done to get it working again. With a hint of pride, I also told them about my steering idea.

Mom said, "Don't you go riding on that thing on Stump Road! There's too much traffic and you'll get run over."

"Yes, Mom," was all I said. The thought had never entered my mind about riding on the buggy up and down Stump Road. Mom sure could be overprotective.

After lunch I had to pick up the toys in the sandbox, put them in a soap box, and carry them to the front cellar room. Picking up after younger brothers and sisters was one of my jobs around the house.

Bringing the toy box into the front cellar gave me the creeps. Snakes liked to sun themselves on the rock wall just before the door on cool days and lay on the ledge just inside the front cellar room on hot days. I learned that if I didn't look around and dilly-dally, I could be in and out of the room without seeing anything. A few times I heard something slithering around in the dim room and got out of there really fast.

That chore done, and with no further chores to do, I went back up to Pete's to see what was going on.

I wasn't surprised to see eight boys standing around the buggy. They were walking around it and talking. Dick Kulle even kicked one of the wheels like a man checking over a used car. It's a good thing he didn't kick one of the twine-repaired spokes. It might have broken in two or just fallen off the wheel.

Everybody but the youngest kids got to ride and steer while the rest of us pushed. Pete even let the little kids ride on the buckboards behind the seat.

One of the boys thought the buggy would be more fun if it was on the road. Before anyone could answer, I thought about what Mom had said: How could she know about taking the buggy on the road?

I didn't say anything as the rest of the crowd agreed that it was a grand idea.

Without hesitating, Pete got up on the seat and the gang pushed the buggy out to the road. I just stood there feeling trapped between Mom's words and being left out of some great fun.

Someone yelled back to me, "Aren't you going to help, Mike?"

Not wanting to look lazy, I ran to catch up and pushed with the other boys. I remembered Mom's words: "Don't you go riding that thing on Stump Road!"

I felt better because I wasn't riding—I was pushing.

Pete had made a right turn out of his driveway and was heading west. I caught up with the buggy just as it got in front of the Pinker house.

We were going at a fast pace as Pete turned left onto County Line Road and headed up the hill. Our speed went down quickly. We all had to shift our muscles into a lower gear because of the hill and the stone road.

When we got to the top of the hill, we were all panting like dogs. Pete noticed, took pity, and told us to stop. On occasion, Pete could be very thoughtful.

As we leaned against the wheels or the buckboards catching our breaths, I noticed that Pete was looking down the road. I followed his gaze to Mudcoe Hill. It was almost half a mile away. The hill went up the rocky road at a very steep angle. It was even steeper than Vinegar Hill, but it wasn't quite as long.

I wasn't having a good feeling because I had witnessed Pete's daring while sledding in Beaver Meadow.

When our panting had decreased but was not entirely gone, Pete said to no one in particular, "How would you like to take a ride down Mudcoe Hill?"

There was dead silence.

"Come on, guys. It will be great fun." Pete said this with joy and a hint of madness in his voice.

Silence again.

Davey finally said, "Okay, but I don't think we can push the buggy all the way up the hill. How about going up halfway?"

After a pause, Pete replied, "I guess that will be far enough. Let's get moving."

Pete grabbed the twine and we were off at a quick trot because it was a slight, downhill grade almost all the way to where County Line is intersected by Sheldon and Miller Roads.

Like any good driver, Pete had us stop the buggy at the stop sign. He let us rest for a bit before the final push up to the middle of the steep hill.

I walked around slowly with my hands on my hips catching my breath. No one was talking except Pete because the rest of us didn't have our wind back yet.

I looked over at the old abandoned Mudcoe School house and wondered how it would be if I went to school in a room with kids from kindergarten on up through high school.

Some of the boys started talking, and Pete took this as a sign that we were all back to a normal operating condition.

"Let's go, guys. Don't push fast. Save your energy."

Pete could be very considerate.

The pushing was pretty easy because the grade was very gentle for a good two hundred feet. After that, the going got very tough.

Pete gave us another break.

We had to lean against the buggy so it wouldn't roll back down the hill.

To help us out, Pete got down from his seat, went over to the ditch, and found a large, flat stone to place behind one of the back wheels.

By this time I was regretting the way I fine-tuned Mom's words to get around what she had really meant.

Pete was looking up the hill again with a furrowed brow as if he was in deep thought.

I got a really bad feeling and decided that I would rather be back home dealing with snakes in the cellar.

"You know, guys. We're not that far from the top. &*$$, we've come this far, why not go all the way to the top?" Pete said this slowly and had added the cuss word for effect.

Again, nobody said a word.

Pete was staring at us.

I knew he saw a combination of fear and exhaustion in all of us. We all avoided his stare by looking down at our sneakers.

I looked up a bit and saw Pete shaking his head in a way that expressed both disgust and disappointment. He then turned his back to us, walked to the front of the buggy, picked up the steering twine, and began to pull the buggy slowly up the hill.

He hadn't moved the buggy more than a few feet before Davey put his hands on the back of the thing and began pushing. Without thinking, the rest of us did the same.

The buggy moved much easier without Pete's weight on it, but by the time we were nearing the top, some of us were pulling on the big wheels while the rest were pushing at the back of the wagon.

Pete was the only one standing by the time we got to the top. The rest of us were sprawled out on the grass along both sides of the road.

It took a very long time before we were rested enough to even pick ourselves up off the grass. Pete then had us turn the buggy so it was facing downhill.

From the top of Mudcoe Hill we could see all the way to the huge drumlins just before Jordan, a good three miles as the crow flies.

Looking down the hill was a frightening thing. It seemed even steeper now than it did when I rode down it in a car. I also noticed for the first time that there were deep ditches on either side of the road.

One of the boys, I won't mention his name because I don't want to embarrass him, looked like he peed in his pants a bit. I know I wasn't far behind that stage of fear myself.

"There are too many of us for the wagon to hold." Pete said with sadness in his voice. He continued, "That's a shame because it took all of us to get the buggy to the top."

One of the younger boys, Corky Sheridan, was smart. He said, "It's only fair that the older boys get to ride down because they did most of the work."

Pete said, "Good thinking, Corky. What do you guys say?"

The younger boys chimed in at the same time that it was a great idea.

Pete looked at us. No one dared to say he didn't want to get on the wagon, so in Pete's mind it was settled.

My last hope was that the wagon wouldn't hold the remaining numbers of those condemned, or I would be considered one of the younger boys.

It didn't work. I was the last one to make the cut-off to call it a full load. I found myself sitting with my back to the front of the wagon with my legs dangling over the back edge because the rest of the small wagon floor was packed. Pete decided that he couldn't handle the steering by himself, so he had Davey sit with him on the seat to handle the right-side steering twine. Davey sure didn't look too thrilled about his assignment.

Pete gave the word for the younger boys to give the buggy a small push to get it moving and told those of us on the wagon to hold on tight.

As we started to pick up speed, Pete yelled in an excited voice, "Hold onto your britches, boys, she's going to buck!"

My hands were tightly gripping the edges of the boards, but my rear end was still lifting off the wood every time the wagon hit a big stone. I looked down and noticed the gravel going by in an ever increasing blur.

I could tell Pete and Davey were having trouble with the steering because the buggy was going from one side of the road to the other barely missing disaster.

On one extra sharp swerve, a crew member either got thrown out or decided to bail out to save himself. He tumbled two or three times before he went into the ditch. When he stopped, all I could see was a foot sticking up into the air.

It was fortunate that Davey and Pete got their steering act together because we would have surely died a terrible death if they hadn't.

By the time the hill started to flatten out, we were going faster than the speed limit in Skaneateles Falls, two of the boards had fallen off becoming splinters on the road as they flipped over and over, and a piece of loose bailing twine was hitting my face every time the wheel next to me made a turn.

We had gained so much speed that we zoomed right through the stop sign at the intersection and came to a halt a good way past it.

I could faintly hear the boys yelling and cheering as they came running down the hill. By the time they got to the boy who ended up in the ditch, he was slowly climbing up its bank, brushing himself off, and checking for damage.

None of us moved. We were all enjoying the calm after the storm. The silence was almost deafening after the loud, bone-rattling ride we had just survived.

I realized that I still had a very strong grip on the edges of the wood, relaxed my fingers, and finally took my first conscious breath.

The younger boys arrived on the scene and started running around the buggy in a strange victory dance with lots of yelling and jibber-jabber.

As if on cue, we all got off the wagon and looked at each other. We started to smile and then laugh.

We had lived through something—something we had no right to live through—and we all knew it.

On the way back to Pete's house, we were all talking about the things that had happened to us. Everyone got a good laugh when I told them about the bailing twine hitting my face.

After awhile, we all went silent, except for the smaller boys. We were all in our own deep thoughts.

Mine came to angels. There must have been a ton of them hovering right over our heads as we went down the hill.

It didn't take long for word to spread around the area about our ride. Mom found out in short order that I was one of the riders. I didn't even bother to try to argue my case because I knew I had been disobedient. I wasn't allowed to leave the yard after school for a whole week.

BEAVER MEADOW: PART II

Beaver Meadow was our local, giant playground. It had been used as pasture land for many years because the bedrock was too close to the surface and the hills too steep for either horses or tractors to work the meager soil.

Dad told me that he had played cowboys and Indians, swam in its stream holes, drank from its springs, and been chased by the bulls in Beaver Meadow. He also said trout were in the stream until water snakes came in and ate them all up.

The only "real" playground in all of Skaneateles Falls was at the old school. There were some swings, a baseball field, and a good-sized slide. That was fine for younger kids who lived close to the school, but not useful to the rest of the small kids in the community. Most moms were too busy doing housework to take time to walk their little ones to the school playground.

In Stump City we made use of rope swings, dirt boxes, and other imaginative things to keep ourselves busy and from under foot in the house.

Besides my father telling me about Beaver Meadow, I learned how much fun it was to play there from the older kids.

My first solo venture there was very scary because Mr. Peter's bull was always somewhere in the fenced meadow from early spring to late fall. The bull and the heifers were hard to spot because bushes more than big enough to hide them had grown up in the meadow over the years.

The heifers didn't bother me at all because I was used to being around them at the Olmstead farm. On the other hand, I had a healthy respect for bulls because of what I had seen when

I went there with Dad. The Olmstead bull was kept inside most of the time in a thick, steel-barred pen. Anytime it was taken outside, a rope was attached to the ring in his nose to control him. Dad always put me in a safe place when he and Johnny Olmstead took the bull out. Johnny led him with the rope, and Dad armed himself with a pitch fork to keep the bull moving in the right direction in a fairly well-mannered fashion.

Once a year or so, Dad would hear about some farmer who'd been either gored by a bull and injured or been killed.

With my knowledge of bulls firmly and permanently imbedded in my brain, I went on my first adventure to Beaver Meadow.

When I got to the edge of the meadow I looked over the fence for any sign of danger. I didn't see or hear anything, so I climbed through an opening between two strands of barbed wire. Once on the other side, I stood still and put my senses on high alert for anything out of the ordinary.

Sensing none, I started walking down the same steep hill we had gone sledding on. I saw a good sized stick and armed myself with it.

I quickly learned to make sure that there was no bull on the other side of a bushy area by peeking around the edge. I used the same technique every time I came to a big bush.

I was walking along a flat section in the valley part of the meadow when I saw a very green area. I walked over to see what it was. The grass was growing in mud. Walking around it, I found where the water was coming from. It was a small spring.

I was pretty thirsty. I looked around for any sign of the bull before I bent down to cup the cool water into my hands. It tasted very good, so I drank my full.

I walked only a minute longer when something white caught my eye on the hill at the other end of the meadow. I froze and looked more closely. Just then something at one end of the white spot flashed when it caught the sun's rays just right. It was the bull! His nose ring had flashed in the light. I felt a sense of relief because I now knew exactly where he was.

Keeping one eye on the bull and one eye on where I was walking, I moved along without really knowing where I was headed. I saw more green a short distance in front of me and walked towards it. It was the bank of the stream.

The stream wasn't very wide or deep and was flowing very slowly. I followed it downstream and came upon the swimming hole Dad had talked about. It was pretty wide and a good four feet deep. I took off my well-worn Keds sneakers and holey socks. The water felt cool and refreshing. I started kicking my feet in the water and made lots of noise. I stopped suddenly when I thought of the bull.

I had found two spots that Dad talked about and tried to imagine him as a kid my age drinking the spring water and playing in the swimming hole. I just couldn't do it. Dad had always been Dad and seeing him at my age, other than in pictures, was impossible for my brain to do.

After letting my feet dry in the air for a few minutes, I put my socks and sneakers back on. I walked away from the swimming hole and looked back to mark its spot in my brain just like I had marked the spot of the spring.

On the way back, I looked over my shoulder once in awhile to make sure the bull was still on the other hill. He was. As I got closer to the fence, I stopped looking and concentrated on climbing back up the steep sledding hill. I had my head down and was leaning against the hill when a heifer suddenly came out from behind a bush. I almost wet my pants before I realized I was in no danger.

I climbed back through the fence and headed back home vowing to myself that I would be back to explore and play again in Beaver Meadow.

FOOLED BY MR. PINKER

Suffering through a very sticky, warm afternoon, I slowly shuffled up Stump Road. It was rarely quiet in Stump City unless the Waltons were out of town, and they were. All but a few of them had stuffed themselves into the family sedan and headed to Auburn to visit Mrs. Walton's sister and her family. Davey told me that his aunt had many children too.

I knew Peter, the oldest Walton boy, was home because his little MG convertible was parked under one of the huge maples in the front yard. His car was even better looking than Uncle Jimmy's woody wagon. Peter always put a smart, short-brimmed hat on before he went driving. He must have thought that it gave him a dashing look. Davey thought otherwise and laughed at him behind his back.

Anyway, I was just getting past their house when I saw Bobby Kulle coming out of his front door.

"Hi, Bobby. What's going on?" I said.

"Not much. I have to go to Grandpa's and help Grandma move something in the kitchen. Do you want to come along?"

I hesitated for a moment because the memory of almost getting caught stealing his Grandpa's grapes came racing back into my head.

"Okay," I half-heartedly replied.

Because of the sticky heat, we took our time walking up the road and didn't talk much. We were only a few feet onto Mr. Pinker's lawn when I heard Rusty barking and saw him lamely charging around the side of the house towards us. I froze thinking he would surely attack me.

When he got close to Bobby, he said, "Hi, Rusty."

Rusty's look instantly changed and his tail began to wag.

Bobby reached down and started petting him. "Nice doggie," Bobby said as if he was talking to a baby.

Bobby looked up at me and said, "Pet him and talk like I did. He really likes it."

I slowly put my hand on Rusty's haunches expecting him to suddenly turn back to the Rusty I'd learned to fear. Then I started talking like I did to whoever the baby-of-the-moment was in our house.

To my great relief, Rusty loved it.

Rusty led us to the back of the house. It was the first time I'd ever been there.

I looked around the backyard at the well-kept vegetable and flower gardens. While I was looking, I got a start when I heard Mr. Pinker's voice coming from inside his grape arbor.

"Bobby, Bobby. How's my Bobby?" He said in his heavily foreign accent.

"I'm fine, Grandpa," Bobby said as we entered the arbor.

Bobby went over to his grandpa who was seated in a long chair swing hanging from the top of the arbor. His grandpa patted him on the back.

Mr. Pinker looked at me and Bobby said, "Grandpa, this is Michael Quigley. He lives on the street behind Welch Allyn."

Mr. Pinker looked at me, smiled, and said, "I know who you are, Michael."

He gave me a look that told me that he not only knew me, but he also knew what I had done, or was I just feeling guilty?

Bobby said to both his grandpa and me, "I'm going inside to help Grandma. I'll be back soon."

I was scared and stood there looking down without saying a word.

"Sit down, Michael. Sit down here." He was patting the empty space next to him on the swing.

"Yes, sir," I said as I slowly went over to sit next to him.

I sat there for a few minutes looking straight ahead as he rocked us back and forth. I thought for sure he would grab me by the neck at any second, but he didn't.

The awkward silence was getting to me, so I said, "You sure have a beautiful backyard, Mr. Pinker. I can't believe how much cooler it is under the grape leaves."

"Thank you, Michael. We work very hard to keep it nice."

I didn't know what to say. I was beginning to feel sorry about stealing his grapes and ruining some vines while escaping.

"Did you know that just about every year when the grapes are ripe, at least one boy climbs over the fence right over there and steals grapes?" He said this with his finger coming up to mark the exact spot where we had climbed.

"Really, Mr. Pinker?" I tried to say this with surprise in my voice, but I felt like I had come up well short.

"Yes, indeed, Michael. Yes, indeed." He said.

There was a pause and then with a smile coming to his face he added, "I planted extra grapevines over there to keep the boys from getting past them and into the really good grapes."

I couldn't continue my poor acting and think I gave myself away with the surprised look on my face.

He smiled even more when he said, "Rusty and me have a great time scaring the boys half to death. Why, Rusty wouldn't hurt a flea, and I'm too old to go chasing boys around in the dark."

He had just finished speaking when Bobby came out of the house.

"I'm all done, Mike. Do you want to go back to my place and play some catch?"

"Sure," I said.

As I got up to go, Mr. Pinker said with a twinkle in his eyes, "Michael, it was good talking to you. I'd give you some grapes, but they're not in season."

I smiled back at him and said, "It was fun talking to you, Mr. Pinker."

As Bobby and I were leaving, I turned around and gave a quick wave to Mr. Pinker. He just winked back.

I wondered if Mr. Pinker had more fun scaring us half to death than we had stealing his grapes.

THE BOOB TUBE AFFECTS ME: *PART II*

During the good weather, I didn't watch much television because Mom kicked all us old enough to play on our own out of the house in order to get her chores done in some semblance of peace.

It was a rainy Saturday afternoon and most of us kids were sitting around watching the tube. During advertisements, we horsed around some but settled back down once the show we happened to be watching started up again.

We were sitting there when it was announced that a Tarzan movie would be coming on at the start of the next hour.

I heard about Tarzan and how he swung through the jungle on vines, but I had never seen him do it.

We all loved the movie. It was loaded with all kinds of action. We really got excited when Tarzan swam as fast as he could to barely avoid the jaws of a huge crocodile.

I paid serious attention whenever he started swinging from vine to vine. It was a beautiful thing to see. He made it look so easy.

A week or so after the movie I was sitting on the front steps with my hands holding up my head wondering what I could do. I was really bored because nobody was around to play with. I suddenly focused on the woods across the street.

I had lost interest in going there because Dad had finally found out about my tree chopping and put a quick end to my fun. He also added a good dose of redness to my behind for added effect.

It suddenly dawned on me that I had seen huge wild grape vines growing somewhere in the woods when I was looking for good trees to chop down. During past travels across the street I hadn't paid that much attention to them, so I couldn't remember how high up in the trees they grew or exactly where I had seen them.

I went back into the house and said, "Mom, is it okay for me to go play in the woods?"

Mom said the usual, "Don't go in the water or on steep banks." She then added something new, "Leave the axe in the shed."

She had all known bases covered except one. She didn't say, "Leave the pruning saw in the shed."

"Okay, Mom," I said as I went out the front door and used the same method to get the saw as I used to get the axe.

Once safely in the woods with the saw, I used the 'zig and zag' way of looking for the grapevines. It took some time before I found a mess of vines just before the Bennett property at the end of our road.

All of the vines were a good two inches thick and went way up into the trees. I started sawing the vines about a foot up from the ground. It was hard work because the saw kept binding up. I cut four of them and decided that would be enough for a young Tarzan.

I walked back up the hill to the first one I cut, grabbed it, walked backward, and then ran forward. I went swinging out over the slope and reached for the next vine. I got enough of it to wrap my right hand around and let go of the first one. My grip wasn't good enough, and I hit the ground with a thud. It hurt, but not enough to keep me from trying again.

I hit the ground with a thud five more times before I held onto the second vine. I had done it!

There was only one problem, the second vine didn't swing out far enough for me to even get close to the third vine, and I had to let myself drop to the ground.

Standing there in deep thought didn't help me find an answer to the problem, so I went back up the hill to get the pruning saw.

All the way home I put different ideas through my head, but nothing came to me that might work.

At least I had gone from one vine to another.

Many days later, I finally thought of something that might work and asked Mom if I could go into the woods.

Again, she went through her list of "don'ts" and let me go.

I didn't need the pruning saw, so I went straight down the road and turned into the woods near the area where I had cut the vines.

Ignoring the first two vines, I walked down to the third one. I found a dead branch and picked it up. I grabbed the bottom of the vine and pulled it back up the hill. It took some doing, but I finally got the branch stuck into the ground. Then I laid the bottom of the vine over the branch.

I went back up the hill to the first vine, grabbed it, walked backwards to a spot that would give me enough swing to reach the second vine, and ran forward. I went flying, grabbed the next vine, let go of it at the right time, and was off swinging towards the third one.

It worked!

I held on for dear life as I swished toward the fourth vine. It was way out of my reach, so I let myself swing back and dropped to the ground.

I propped the fourth vine back with a branch, did the same thing to the third one, and walked back to the top.

Before I took off, I took a deep breath and looked down the hill to make sure all the vines were in the right position.

I didn't realize I was picking up more speed with each vine, and before I could reach out to grab the fourth vine, I went zooming by it. I just couldn't seem to make my hand move fast enough to grab the vine as I went passed it.

I kept trying until my hands were raw, but just couldn't get my timing right to grab the fourth vine. I left the woods feeling happy my idea had worked, but frustrated that I couldn't make a complete run.

It took many more trips into the woods before the fourth vine was conquered. My hands were all calloused and my arms a bit bigger from all my efforts.

Not being satisfied, I cut vines all the way down to the bottom of the hill with the last one no more than ten feet from the bank of the creek.

I went swinging down the hill yelling like Tarzan. A few times I made it to the last vine and went way out over the creek.

Oh, what a feeling!

I didn't dare tell anyone about the vines because Mom would surely find out and my Tarzan days would be over and my butt reddened again. But the day came when I couldn't keep my secret to myself any longer.

I told my sister, Terry.

She got all excited when I told her and immediately went into the house to ask Mom if she could go into the woods with me.

Mom said it would be okay for her to go as long as I was with her.

When we got to the vines, I showed Terry the line of vines. She watched me swing from one to the other and instantly decided that she could do it too. I didn't bother trying to argue with her because once she put her mind on doing something, I was just wasting my breath trying to talk her out of it. Without saying anything, I handed her the vine and stood to the side.

On her very first attempt she missed just like I did, but came down on her stomach instead of her feet. The wind instantly came out of her lungs. She turned all kinds of colors before she got enough air in her lungs to start bawling loudly.

After I did my clumsy best to calm her down some, I brushed the dirt and dead leaves off her clothes. On the way back home, I made her promise not to say anything to Mom or Dad.

She didn't tell on me, and she didn't want to try being Jane anymore. She did watch me being Tarzan once in awhile.

A time came when I was swinging through the vines and decided I'd really be like Tarzan. Looking around to make sure no one was in the area, I took off all my clothes except my underpants, and made several runs down the hill. After a few more runs, I had to stop because the rough grape bark was scratching up my skin and causing it to bleed in spots.

Within a day, I started itching on the inside of my legs and all the way up to the right side of my chest. At first I thought it was just the scratches from the bark, but the itching got worse instead of better.

I went into the bathroom. After I closed the door I took off my shirt and pants. I had a very nasty looking red streak running in almost a straight line from the middle of my chest all the way down to the bottom of my calves.

I got worried but not as worried as I got when I stretched open the top of my underpants. No! I had it there too! My heart was pounding in my chest and a cold sweat was breaking out on my forehead.

I quickly got dressed and ran into the kitchen.

"Mom, Mom, I'm going to die!"

"Michael, Michael. We're all going to die." She never even turned her head away from the sink nor stopped scrubbing the cast iron frying pan.

"But Mom, I am!" I wailed and started sobbing.

Mom now knew something serious was going on.

She dropped the pan into the sink and turned around quickly saying, "What is the matter?"

"Look at this, Mom!" I was pulling my T-shirt over my head as I was talking.

"Holy Mary, Mother of....! What have you gone and gotten yourself into?" She said this with passion and deep concern, which only made me more afraid.

I wailed, "I have the same thing on my legs, and, and, on my private parts."

"Vinnie, Vinnie. Come here quickly." Mom yelled out through the back screen door.

Dad came flying through the door knowing the tone of Mom's voice meant trouble.

Mom pointed to me and said, "Look at him! Look at him!"

Dad walked over, got really close, and looked at my chest.

He looked again and said, "That's one good dose of poison ivy you've gotten."

He then turned to Mom and calmly said, "Get the Calamine lotion."

"But, Vinnie, he even has it on his private parts."

"You'd better forget the lotion. I think it wise to take him to Doc Horn's. Go over to Helen's and make the call."

He then turned to me and said, "You'll be okay, son, but you need to see Doc Horn to be on the safe side."

Mom came back in with Helen right behind her.

Helen said, "Be gone. Be gone the three of ya.. I'll watch the wee uns."

Mom and Dad got into the front seat and I got into the back one. I wasn't as scared now because I knew poison ivy didn't kill very many kids—at least all of the ones I knew who got it had not died.

It didn't take long at all to get to Doc Horn's office in Skaneateles.

He was waiting at the front door of his house and took us all into his office.

Doc Horne parachuted into France on D-Day to take care of the wounded. He was tough and survived the invasion without much harm done, so it took a lot to bother him when it came to broken body parts and sickness.

He said, "What have you gotten yourself into, Michael? Take off all your clothes."

I didn't dare object, so I did as I was told.

Mom and Dad were both shocked to see the way I was covered with the itchy stuff.

Doc Horne was looking at me with curiosity written all over his face. "How did you get the poison ivy in such a nice, neat line running up and down your body?"

It suddenly dawned on me how it had happened.

As quietly as I could and with my head lowered, I said, "I was swinging on vines in the woods with just my underpants on."

"I see. And when were you playing Tarzan in your underpants?" He asked this, but I could see he was trying to keep from laughing.

"The day before yesterday, Doctor Horne."

"Well, I'll give you a bottle of Calamine lotion to take home with you. It's very important that you keep from itching yourself. That will only cause the poison to spread all over your body." He said this in a very serious, no-nonsense tone.

"Yes, Doctor. I won't scratch myself."

He turned and said to Dad, "Vinnie, you've got your hands full."

Dad said, "Bob, I sure do."

I was told to get dressed and Doc Horne gave Mom the bottle of lotion. He also told her how I should be washed to help keep the poison from spreading.

Mom and Dad thanked Doc Horne as we left the office.

On the way home there was silence until we were past Mottville.

Dad said, "Michael, I sure hope you had fun swinging on the vines because you are going to be suffering for a few days."

I did, indeed, suffer for a few days.

Apparently Dad thought I went through enough because I never did get punished after I healed.

My Tarzan days were over. From then on, I stayed clear of grape vines just like a smart dog stays away from a skunk after it has sprayed him in the eyes.

THE O'HARA HOME

As mentioned earlier, the O'Hara homestead was on County Line Road. Mr. O'Hara kept the house and small barn behind it in good repair. Mrs. O'Hara kept the inside of her house in even better condition.

The few times that I was on their property I went with Dad. There was no way on earth I'd ever go there without him. Bullet would surely chew me up and spit me out if I did. There definitely wasn't any love lost between the two of us.

Dad always had a way with animals. I don't know if it was the tone of voice he used with them or that they could sense he was someone not to fool with.

On a warm, spring day I had my bicycle tipped upside down and was attaching baseball cards to the spokes with clothespins. They made a great sound when I rode the bike.

Dad came out of the house and said, "Michael, how would you like to walk over to the O'Hara home with me? I have to talk to Mr. O'Hara."

"Sure. I'll finish putting the cards on when we get back."

We made small talk as we walked across the field behind our house and arrived in front of the O'Hara house in short order.

Bullet came out to greet us by showing his teeth and the hair up on his back.

Dad said in a deep, commanding voice, "Bullet. Back." Bullet stopped, turned around and kept his distance.

With one eye on Bullet, I stood there listening to Dad and

Mr. O'Hara exchange thoughts. It was hard to concentrate on what they were talking about because of the dog. This bothered me because they always got around to talking about something interesting that happened years ago.

One thing from the past they mentioned really got my curiosity up. All I caught from the conversation was "Waterbury, almost falling, tower, and dark," with other words like "couldn't see, chased, spilled paint, and slipping," popping up here and there.

I didn't have time to figure out what they were talking about because Mrs. O'Hara stuck her head around the side of the front porch and said, "Michael, come in here and have a glass of milk and a cookie or two."

Now I was in a pickle. On one side there was the Guernsey milk from the cow Mr. O'Hara kept, combined with Mrs. O'Hara's much talked about baking power. On the other side, I'd have to leave the protection Dad offered from Bullet. Do I chance getting bitten for a very special treat?

"That would be great, Mrs. O'Hara. I'll be in shortly." Food quickly conquered fear.

Dad stopped talking at the sound of Mrs. O'Hara's voice, so I had the chance to say, "Is it okay for me to go inside and get a snack?"

"Yes, son," he said and turned to Bullet. "Bullet. Stay!"

Bullet stayed, and I got into the house in short order.

Mrs. O'Hara was short, plump, and very friendly. Her graying hair was tied back in a bun, and her apron had some white flour dust on it. The sparkle in her eyes made her look young.

"It's good to see you, Michael. How is your mother doing?"

She asked this because she knew Mom was shortly due to take a five day vacation at the hospital to have another baby and have a breather from all the work she constantly did around the house.

"Mom is doing fine, Mrs. O'Hara. She told me to ask about you anytime I saw you."

"Tell your Mom that everything is grand here. And tell her thank you for asking." She said this as she got milk out of her new refrigerator and put two beautiful looking oatmeal cookies on a plate.

I remembered my manners and said the right things.

While I munched on the cookies, Mrs. O'Hara sat at the other end of the table talking about people in the neighborhood.

I sat there nodding because I didn't want to answer with a piece of cookie in my mouth.

Mouth empty, I asked, "How are Donny and Dicky doing?"

"Why, they are in the barn right now working on some old car they just got. When you are finished, you can go talk to them if you like."

This surprised me because I hadn't heard any noise coming from the barn while I was half listening to Dad and Mr. O'Hara and keeping an eye on Bullet. Come to think of it, maybe that's why I hadn't heard the boys.

I didn't really know them because they hung around with a much older crowd. But, I had heard some fantastic stories about the trouble they'd gotten themselves into and how tough they were. Most of the boys around my age feared them and kept their distance.

I took my time finishing my cookies and milk because I didn't really want to go talk to them. What could I say to them?

When I finished and got up from the table, I said, "Thank you, Mrs. O'Hara. The milk and cookies were great."

"Oh, you're more than welcome, Michael," she said with a

nice smile and continued, "Just go out the back door and into the barn."

How was I going to get to the barn without Dad there to control Bullet?

Coming up with an idea that might work, I put it into motion.

"Dad, I'm coming out the back door now." I yelled through the screened door.

"Okay, son. Stay, Bullet!"

I quickly ran to the barn and looked behind me. Bullet hadn't moved from the spot he had gone to when Dad and I first arrived.

Donny and Dicky were working on a rusted old car. One of them was leaning over a fender working on the engine and the other was under the car with just his legs sticking out.

I must have startled the both of them because when I said my greeting, they both jumped. The one under the hood came up fast and hit his head on the hood, and the other one's feet went up into the air.

"%4*#&," the one under the hood yelled.

"%*@ $%! ^+," said the other.

I wasn't off to a good start.

"It's me, Michael Quigley."

The one working on the engine turned while rubbing his head. It was Dicky. Donny pulled himself out from under the car.

I tried to smooth over what had happened by saying, "This sure is a swell car."

"Thanks. And don't go sneaking up on us like that!" Donny said while rubbing his forehead.

"Sorry," was all I could mumble. Continuing on, I said, "Do you have it running yet?"

"No, but we're getting close," said Dicky.

Thinking of nothing else to say, I said, "Can I help?"

"Sure. After I get back under the car, when I call for a tool, hand it to me." Donny said while getting down on the dirt floor and crawling back under.

I did as I was told and handed Donny box wrenches, a screwdriver, and a pair of pliers when asked. This went on until Dad called for me to come.

"See ya, guys," I said.

"Thanks for the help," said Donny.

"So long," said Dicky's muffled voice from deep down inside the engine.

During all the time in the barn, I was very tense. Based on their reputation, I was waiting for the other shoe to drop.

Between Bullet and the boys, it wasn't the easiest visit I ever had. The only thing that saved the time there was Mrs. O'Hara's cookies and milk.

I figured that the boys were behaving because they were afraid of what their father and Dad would do to them if they went after me.

Reputation, the rumor mill, and exaggeration swirled around the O'Hara boys. The "swirling" talk about them was always there and never died down. It was something like the way field corn grows on a hot, sunny day after a good, soaking rain.

ROBERTA STAPLES AND KING

I was still carrying the milk from the Staples' farm. My body had adjusted to the pail, and the chore was completed in less than fifteen minutes.

Once in awhile I'd see Roberta helping her dad with the milking and I'd say hello to her.

When working in the barn, Roberta always kept her hair in long braids and was dressed in her work clothes: Clothes that had to be taken off in the back room of the house before her mom would let her go into the kitchen.

Roberta treated me kindly. I instantly liked her for it. She was a shy girl and a few grades ahead of me at Elbridge Central. When I saw her tossing hay bales around, I developed a healthy respect for her. Most boys her age or older couldn't handle the bales as easily as she could. Roberta liked all kinds of animals and was good around them.

Her greatest love was King, a gentle giant of a horse. Ross Caddy had either sold or given King to her father many years earlier. Dad remember King being on the Caddy farm when he worked there as a boy. He said Mr. Caddy bought King from someone out West and shipped him back here by train. Dad also said King had been a working cowpony and in his prime was used for herding and corralling cattle.

Just the thought that a cowboy actually rode on King's back got my imagination going. Cowboy shows on radio and television were always some of the most popular with both youngsters and their parents.

When I knew King was pastured in the field close to the milk house, I looked for him before I took the milk pail into the shed. If he wasn't too far down the field, I called his name and he came trotting up to greet me. I reached carefully over the electric fence to pet his soft muzzle and scratch behind his ears. He'd stand there making soft, horse sounds while he looked me straight in the eye. I rewarded his patience by giving him some fresh grass from my side of the fence. If Mom had a carrot end or one a bit on the soft side, I'd carry it down with me and pull it out of my back pocket. I made sure to put the treat in my palm the way Dad had shown me, and King would lip it off leaving all of my fingers attached to my hand.

My sister, Terry, loved horses and became good friends with Roberta. When she didn't have to keep an eye on one of our younger brothers or sister, she'd either be at the Staples' farm or up the road helping Charlotte Walters take care of her horses.

I did venture to the Staples' farm a few times with Terry and helped the girls brush King. Sometimes all three of us got on a fence rail or a huge stone and climbed aboard his high, broad, bare back.

Once we were loaded on, Roberta took us into the fields behind the barns and we rode around. Roberta steered King with just a rope attached to his halter. If she put the rope across the left side of his neck, King went to the right. When she wanted him to go to the left, she put the rope across the right side of his neck. To stop, she just said, "Whoa." To go faster than a walk, she gently put her heels into his sides and we went faster.

With three of us on his back, it was hard to stay aboard when King started to trot. Our up and down motions wouldn't be the same, and once Terry or me began to slip to one side and started falling, the other two soon followed.

We never got hurt in a spill, but once in awhile one of us landed in a cow plop.

While we got ourselves up, King stood close with his head down looking at us. It was almost as if he was checking to be sure we were okay.

Roberta never put the horse into a gallop with three of us aboard because it was too dangerous. After Terry and I slid off the horse when we got back from a ride, she turned the horse, put her heals harder into King's sides and said, "Go!"

King took off like a shot out of a cannon. Within a matter of seconds, his head was straight out and Roberta's chest was almost touching his outstretched neck with her head halfway up it.

Watching them working together was a beautiful sight filled with fading sound. Roberta and the horse were in a single, smooth motion. His tail was straight out behind him, and Roberta's long braids were behind her head flapping on her back. Dirt was kicked high into the air, and the thunderous sounds of the huge animal's hoofs pounding hard into the pasture slowly faded but did not totally vanish.

When the team, for that is what they were, got close to the end of the field, they slowed down just enough to make a sharp turn. Both leaned over at the same steep angle and quickly gained speed as they straightened up and headed for home.

When they got closer, they slowed down just enough to allow for one of those quick stops I saw cowboys do with their horses either on TV or in the movies.

Standing just in front of us, King and Roberta pulled in air at a fast pace. Roberta sat on the horse grinning from ear-to-ear. King's ears were perked up and he held his head really high while he scraped the ground with his left-front hoof.

It was at the end of a run like this that I figured Roberta was dreaming about being a cowgirl, and King was reliving days gone by.

Roberta was a remarkable rider, and King was a remarkable horse.

PAPER BOY

Dick Kulle, Bobby's older brother, had a newspaper route. The route covered Stump City, the block of houses on School Street, and back down Stump Road to where it intersects Jordan Road. It was a very good moneymaker for him. The Post Standard paid two cents for each daily paper delivered and five cents for each Sunday edition. It was much more for the Sunday paper because it was a lot heavier and more expensive.

The Kulle family was going on vacation for a week, so Dick asked me if I would do the route for him.

I told him that I'd like to if Mom let me.

Mom knew how Dick labored when he carried the Sunday paper in the white, cloth sack with The Post Standard printed on it and didn't know if I could handle the weight. She knew I wasn't nearly as strong as Dick.

She finally gave in after I told her how much I'd make on each paper delivered.

Mom added one last thing. "Just remember that your father needs his rest and won't be getting up with the birds to help you."

I didn't know for certain if I could handle the job but said, "I know I can do it Mom, and I won't ask Dad to help me."

Mom thought a moment and answered me with, "Alright, but I don't want you complaining to me or your father about getting up early and carrying the papers."

With that, I was off to tell Dick I could do the delivering for him.

Dick said, "That's great! Be here by 5:30 tomorrow morning, and I'll show you the route."

Just before I went to bed, I borrowed Dad's alarm clock and slept on the couch like I did when I went fishing with Uncle Jimmy.

The next morning the alarm woke me with a start. I quickly turned it off, got my clothes on, reset the clock, and quietly put it on the nightstand next to Dad's head.

I got to Dick's house a few minutes early, but he was already on his front porch putting the newspaper into the cloth sack.

We greeted each other and he quietly said, "Make sure to bring a pocketknife with you so you can cut the twine on the paper bundle. The route deliveryman puts them on the front porch every morning around five o'clock."

I nodded and helped Dick finish putting the papers into the sack.

Dick said, "Here, put the sack over your shoulder."

Trying to make it look easy, I hoisted the sack by the strap up over my head. I don't think there was enough light for Dick to see my arm shaking as I lifted it, put the strap over my head, and onto my right shoulder.

Could I manage the weight? I was having some serious doubts.

Dick showed me where to put the paper at each house we went to. He stressed that it was important because he didn't want any complaints from his customers about wet papers if it rained, or papers blown all over the place if it was windy.

Memorizing all he had to tell me as we went from house to house took my mind off the many pounds of papers I was hauling. It took almost an hour to finish the route.

When the bag was empty and we were walking back to Dick's house, he said, "I was worried that you couldn't carry the full sack, but you did fine. Do you want to go around again tomorrow to make sure that you got everything straight?"

"I think that would be a good idea."

"Okay. Be here at the same time tomorrow and bring your pocket knife, and I'll show you where the best spot is to cut the twine."

I was there at the appointed time with my pocketknife.

I only goofed up at a few houses and felt confident I could handle the job on my own.

As we were getting close to his house, Dick said, "We're taking off tomorrow morning, so you will start the day after tomorrow."

"Okay. I won't let you down."

I was just getting onto the road when Dick said, "I almost forgot. On Saturday afternoon, you'll have to go around the route and collect money. Wait a second and I'll get the list for you."

Dick went into the house and came back with his list.

He said, "Some people owe money for more than one week, some won't be home, and some won't have the money to pay you."

He showed me how to read the list and where to write "paid" or "owed".

I had a few questions and he answered them for me.

"Mike, do you have it straight in your mind?" Dick showed concern because he knew it was a lot to remember and wanted to make sure I wouldn't mess things up.

"Yes," I said with more confidence in my voice than I had in my brain.

Dick said, "One other thing. Some customers will give you a tip when they pay. The tips are yours to keep."

"Thanks, Dick!"

The big day came and I was at the Kulle house early because I was anxious to get started. The sack was on a porch chair and the bundle of papers in the same spot they had been placed before.

I cut the twine, loaded the sack, hoisted it over my shoulder, and was off. I had to stop and think a few times about where to put a paper and sighed with relief when I remembered.

Each day I delivered, the job became easier and the weight of a full sack seemed to be a little lighter.

On Saturday afternoon I went around the route collecting money. Only a few people weren't home, and just two people told me that they'd have to pay next week. The tips ran from nothing up to a whopping twenty-five cents. I made sure to keep the money for the paper in a small money purse Mom had loaned to me and put the tips in my other pocket.

When I got back home, I first took out the purse and counted the money to make sure it matched the total on the list. That done, I pulled out the change from my pocket, put it on the kitchen table, and counted. I was amazed to find I made over a dollar in tips. Why, it was more than I found when I had dug for treasure in front of the McEneny house in what seemed like many years ago.

I was worried about the weight of the paper sack coming up the next morning, but put it out of my head by thinking about what I might buy with the all the money I was making.

I couldn't believe the size of the bundle on Sunday morning. It was at least three times bigger than any of the other bundles. After jamming the papers into the carrying sack, I tried to lift it over my head and put it on my shoulder like I did with the regular paper but had no luck. I thought for a moment to come up with a plan. I ended up dragging the sack close to the steps, sitting down on the step closest to the porch floor, putting the strap over my shoulder, and standing up with my knees shaking a little with the weight.

My shoulder started to hurt before I got to the end of Kulle's sidewalk and onto the road. Walking with the daily paper hadn't been too hard. Now the weight of the sack pushed against my thigh and made me walk like I was shaped like a sideways U.

By the time I had finished delivering to the houses in Stump City, the strap seemed like it was cutting into my shoulder, my hip was being rubbed raw by the sack, and my wind was quickly leaving me.

I didn't see anyone while I delivered the papers. If someone was up and looking out his window, he would have seen me looking something like a slave in Egypt hauling a huge load on his shoulder.

I rested at the bridge over the creek for a few minutes. I didn't dare take the sack off my shoulder because I knew I'd never be able to hoist it back on again, so I rested it on the bridge wall while I stood there trying to recover.

Halfway down School Street the sack finally reached the weight of a full load of daily papers, but by that time I was almost completely done in.

Strength slowly came back to me when I finished on School Street and was on the home stretch. I only had five or so papers left.

Finally, an empty sack! As I walked down the steep hill by Rodak's Bar, I felt a deep sense of accomplishment. I even had a very slight spring in my step when I turned onto our street.

The last two days on the job went well, and the full load of daily papers didn't bother me at all. I made sure to get the paper sack and money to Dick the afternoon he got back from vacation.

When he answered my knocking at his front door he said, "Thanks, Mike. Did you have any problems?"

"No. Everything went fine." I didn't want to tell him about the trouble I had with the Sunday paper.

"Heck, I thought for sure the Sunday paper would be a problem. I sure had trouble the first few weeks until I got used to it." He added, "How did you do for tips?"

"I made over a dollar in tips. Come to think of it, I got pretty pooped out too." I added it like an afterthought in an attempt to cover up my fib.

"Over a dollar! That's great!"

I took over his route a few more times when the family went on vacation. The route grew some, but the weight never bothered me again like it did the first time.

Maybe I was growing some and getting stronger. Who knows?

WINE INTO WATER

I got used to being an altar boy and doing my assigned routines. I also took up Pete Cashin's mumbling method when I didn't feel like saying the Latin and wasn't positioned too close to the priest. Just like Pete, I never got caught.

It was the altar boys' job to clean up the room behind the altar after each Mass while the priest greeted and talked to people at the front door as they left. It never took long to tidy up because a lady came in once a week to do the cleaning the right way.

On one particular Sunday, Davey was the senior altar boy on duty for the mass. We finished our picking up and had just taken off our altar boy gowns and hung them up.

Davey went very quiet and was acting like he was up to something but wasn't saying anything to me.

He leaned over and whispered, "Mike, go to the side door and see if the priest is still at the back of the church."

I knew enough to not ask any questions and did what I was told.

I stuck my head around the door and looked. The priest was talking to Mrs. Sheridan and Mrs. Phillips.

I walked back to where Davey was waiting and whispered, "He's talking to Mrs. Sheridan." I whispered because Davey had whispered.

"Good. Go back to the door and keep an eye on the priest. If he starts to walk back here, clear your throat. And don't let him see you spying on him."

I didn't know what was going on, but did as I was told. Feeling like some kind of secret agent, I stuck my head around the door just enough to see and watched the priest.

When I heard the tinkling of glass, I turned around to see what was going on. Davey was pulling a wine bottle down from the shelf above the sink. I began to get a sick feeling.

I peeked back around the door again to check on the priest. He was still talking.

I took another quick look at Davey to see what he was up to now. He had his head tilted back and was drinking right out of the wine bottle!

I turned once more to see the priest coming down the aisle towards us. I quickly cleared my throat. Davey got the water running in the sink and added some to the wine bottle.

I quickly left my spot by the door and went back to the clothes rack. Davey was soon next to me making like he had just finished hanging up his altar boy gown. I didn't know what to do, so I did the same.

Father entered the room and said, "Are you boys all done?"

We both said, "Yes, Father," at almost the same time.

"You may go now. Thank you. Be sure to check the schedule on your way out to see when you will be serving again."

We said, "Yes, Father."

When we were outside I was shaking with fear and feeling very guilty..

I hissed, "Davey, Why did you do that?"

A little defensively he said, "Some of the older guys who used to be altar boys told Pete and me that they used to do it. I thought I'd try it too."

"How did it taste?" I asked out of curiosity and thinking the wine must be extra special since it was used for Holy Communion.

"It was good, but Pete must've been drinking the wine before me because it tasted a little watery."

"Weren't you afraid of being caught? Don't you know God is watching everything we do?" I tried to sound holy but failed because Davey knew of some of the things I had done which definitely wouldn't pass muster with God.

"Heck. The older boys told us that even older boys had told them about it." Davey said and added, "For all you know, your father could have done the same thing. Why don't you ask him?"

Davey knew that I'd never dare to ask Dad.

It wasn't more than four weeks later when I did the same thing while Pete stood guard at the door. The holy drink tasted more like grape flavored water than it did wine.

BROKEN GLASSES

My cousin, John Calnon, lived right across the street from Grandma and Grandpa's house. John was over two years younger than me, so I didn't play with him much. My sister, Terry, did play with him a lot because she was born just a few months before he was.

On one of those rare occasions when I played with him, we were having a grand time doing things in his house until his mom, my Aunt Pat, decided that fresh air would be good for us. (I think we were getting a bit loud and wild and she wanted to save the furniture.)

We played some catch, but soon got tired of it. We ended up just standing around like boys do and not saying much when one of us, I can't remember who, thought it would be fun to build a fort in the bushes next to the Pinker fence. We scouted along the fence until we found a real bushy area that looked like it had promise.

We soon had a hole torn through the leafy branches and began burrowing around like two animals making a nest. It wasn't long before we had enough space cleared out to stand up and move around in. We continued expanding our fort on either end by ripping down branches and leaves and sticking them into bare spots to hide our fort from outsiders. We kept on working until we ran out of heavy bushes, and then looked around our fort and congratulated each other on a job well done.

John decided that we ought to clear the stones out and tidy up the place a bit. I agreed, so we set to work.

We were almost done when we heard someone shuffling his feet as he came down Phillips Road.

John parted some branches and whispered to me, "It's Sam Morton."

I had trouble getting along with Sam because he was either real nice or real mean to me. I never knew how he was going to act, so I kept my distance from him.

"What are you guys doing in there?" He said in a gruff, sarcastic voice as he slowly got closer to our fort.

I knew from the tone that it wasn't going to go well.

Sam liked to tease younger kids—the younger the better.

John and I started to walk out of the fort without looking at or answering him. Neither one of us wanted anything to do with Sam and only wanted to be in the safety of John's house.

"Hold on, I want to see what you two have been up to."

He pushed John to the side as he entered our fort.

Well, Well. Isn't this just dandy." Sam said it in a tone that meant just the opposite.

John was upset and said without thinking, "WE think it is."

Sam wasn't used to having a little kid talk to him that way and instantly shoved John down hard onto the dirt floor.

I didn't get mad often, but when I did my fair skin became instantly dark red as my blood quickly reached the boiling point.

I hissed, "Leave him alone, you big bully!"

Sam turned quickly and took a step towards me with his fists balled up.

Without even thinking, I planted my feet and gave him a hard left to the nose just like Dad had shown me.

In an instant Sam was on the ground holding his bloody nose and crying, "Where are my glasses? Where are my glasses?"

My blood was still at the boiling point, and I would have hit him again, but John brought me back to my senses by saying, "We'll find them."

It took the three of us a few moments to find what was left of them. They were twisted in strange angles and the glass was broken in both lenses.

"Wait until I tell my mother what you did. You'll pay for this, Quigley!" Sam said after he had gotten himself out of my range and heading home at a trot.

I yelled back, "You started it!"

This ruined the fun we were having in the fort, so we walked back to the house in silence.

I left for home without going in to say good-bye to Aunt Pat because I didn't want her asking any questions which might lead to what just happened.

Dad was already home from work. I asked him how his day at the office had gone hoping my voice sounded normal.

Dad answered with the usual, "Fine, Michael. How was your day?"

I also answered in the usual way, "It was okay, thanks."

We were just sitting down to eat supper when someone knocked on the kitchen door in an urgent, angry manner.

Mom left the stove to see who it was.

Why, Mrs. Morton, how nice to see you!" I knew Mom was just being polite because she couldn't stomach the woman or her ways.

Without even a polite response, Mrs. Morton got right to the point of her visit, "Ethel, your Michael punched Sam in the nose and broke his glasses." Mom, Dad, and the rest of the crew at the table looked at me.

"Is that true, Michael?" Dad said looking at me right in the eyes.

Everyone was silent waiting for me to answer.

I felt like I was a bad guy on one of the Perry Mason TV shows being questioned by Mason himself. All that was needed were a few more kids at the table to have a jury of twelve.

I swallowed hard and said, "Yes, Dad."

"You see, I told you he did!" The only thing Mrs. Morton didn't do was jump up and down while pointing a finger at me.

Dad stared at Mrs. Morton for a long second before he turned back to me. "Michael, how did you break Sam's glasses?"

I then told the "jury" and the two "lawyers" what happened and why it had happened.

"That's not what Sam told me. Why don't you tell your father the truth?"

It was easy to tell that Dad was getting very hot under the collar. He measured his words before he spoke. "Mrs. Morton, the easiest way to find out who is telling the truth would be for you to go to my sister's house and ask John what happened. Until then, please get out of our house."

Mrs. Morton turned in a big huff with her nose in the air and walked out without saying another word.

After the door closed behind her, Dad turned to me and said, "Michael, is what you told me the God's honest truth?"

Without hesitating I said, "I swear on a Bible it is."

After supper Dad went up to Aunt Pat's to find out what John said to Mrs. Morton.

He came back shortly.

Mom said, "What did Pat tell you?"

"After I got her calmed down a bit, she had John tell her and Mrs. Morton what happened."

"Well, don't keep us in the dark," Mom said sounding a little irritated.

"John told us the exact same thing Michael told us. Sam was lying to his mother."

"That settles that," Mom said as a final note to the story.

"Not exactly," said Dad. "She told Aunt Pat she still wanted Michael to pay $35.00 dollars for a new pair of glasses."

"What! Sam's been wearing those glasses for so long that they look tiny on him." Mom was getting her dander up now.

"Now, Ethel, take it easy. I'm sure Mrs. Morton will come to her senses after she calms down a bit." Dad said in a soft, and not very convincing voice.

"That woman doesn't have any senses!" Mom snapped back.

Dad couldn't argue with that, so he walked out the back door with me following him.

He knew I was behind him and said, "Michael, I'm proud of you for sticking up for your little cousin." He paused, turned, and smiled. "Did you use a solid hook to flatten him?"

"Sure did, Dad." I said while he mussed my hair.

A few days later, Dad got a letter in the mail from Mrs. Morton. She was demanding that he pay her the money for the glasses.

Dad knew she'd take him to court and figured the costs would be much greater, so he mailed her the money.

Paying the money really stuck in his and Mom's craw for a long time, and the pickings were slim at the meal table for several weeks.

MAGAZINE BOY

For some time I had been entrusted with walking to the post office to pick up the mail. Mom had given me the combination to our mailbox and I memorized it.

Mr. Major had retired and Mr. Jackson was now the head of the business. Mr. Jackson and his wife, Ann, lived two houses down from us. They only had two kids, Noni and Donny. I say "only" because a family in Stump City with any number of kids less than four was considered small.

On my trips to the Post Office, once I was over the bridge on Stump Road, I'd take the well-worn cinder path up a small hill and over the steep railroad bank and be almost in front of St. Bridget's. From there, it was a short walk up the road to the Post Office.

Mr. Jackson was a thin, well-organized, gentle man. He always greeted me with a warm smile while looking over the top of his glasses.

If I got there early, I'd stand and watch him sort the mail with quick, deft hands. I can still hear the letters hitting the glass fronts of the mailboxes as he tossed the mail into them.

He was so good that he could even talk while doing it.

Mr. Jackson sometimes relayed to me the latest news in the area that would interest a boy my age, tell me how his weed-free flower beds were doing, and ask me about the family.

When he was done, I'd squat down and check our box for mail. If there was any, I'd open it, get the mail out, and close the box back up. That done, and if Mr. Jackson wasn't talking to someone, I'd say "good-bye" and be on my way.

Shortly after finishing up another week doing Dick Kulle's paper route, I pulled a small magazine out of our mail box. It was a <u>TV Guide</u>.

Why did Mom want a <u>TV Guide</u>? Heck, everyone in the family old enough to talk knew all the facts about the shows from what time they started to what channel they were on. (The channel part was the easiest because we only got two of them.)

When I got home I asked Mom about it.

She looked a bit defensive because she knew how tight money was and buying a magazine, especially one that didn't tell us much more than we already knew, seemed like a waste—even though it was only fifteen cents a week.

"I got it free," she said. "It's what they called a promotion."

"Are we going to buy it?" I asked.

"How can I tell? I haven't looked at it yet." She said with a slight edge to her voice.

She had a good point, a point that made me look foolish, so I shut up, sat at the table, and made a move to open up the magazine.

"Don't you dare! I'll be the first to look at it." Mom said this as if I just tried to open one of her birthday presents.

I quickly took my fingers off it and said, "Sorry, Mom."

I got myself out of the house in a hurry.

When I came back inside from playing, I asked Mom if she had looked through the magazine.

She excitedly told me that she had and thought it was wonderful.

She concluded with, "Why, it even has a crossword puzzle in it!"

Mom loved crossword puzzles and was very good at solving them. When she had a quiet moment, she'd sit at the table and do one to relax and take her mind away from her work and kids.

"Is it okay for me to look through it now?" I asked.

"Yes, you may. But be careful with it. It has the listings for next week's shows and it will have to last."

"I'll be careful with it, Mom." I said as I began thumbing through it as if it was a Bible.

The first thing I did was check for its accuracy. If it didn't have the right times, dates, or channels for shows, I'd know that the magazine was just junk.

It passed that test, so I glanced at the short articles and looked at the ads. I was getting towards the back of it and saw an ad that caught my eye. It said, "Want to make extra money? You can by delivering the TV Guide to your neighbors and friends." It showed a boy about my age with a big smile handing a TV Guide to a lady at her front door.

I said to Mom, "Did you see the ad about delivering the TV Guide?"

"Why, no I didn't. Bring it here and show me."

I walked over to the sink. Mom dried her hands on her apron before she took the magazine from me and looked at the ad.

"That looks interesting," she said.

"Is it okay if I cut the form out of the magazine?" I asked.

"No, not until we are done with it. I don't want it looking bad even before the week's listings in it start." Disappointed, I said that I'd wait.

As soon as the last listing day was finished, I cut the form out, filled it in, and went to the Post Office to mail it.

I told Mr. Jackson what I was doing and he said, "It looks like you want to become an entrepreneur."

Not really knowing what it meant but liking the sound of the word anyway, I said, "Yes, Mr. Jackson."

I was really surprised when I got information back so quickly because I'd filled out forms for free things from cereal box tops when I was smaller, and it would take over a month before I got my free gifts. Most of the stuff was junk, but the thrill of getting something in the mail was always good.

I hurried home with the mail and tore open the package. Once I looked over the directions for delivering and collecting money, I decided that even an idiot could deliver the magazine and make a nice profit.

After showing Mom the information and explaining what I had to do to start and keep a route running, she said it sounded good to her and I could give it a try.

The first thing I had to do was walk around the area and ask people if they wanted the <u>TV Guide</u> delivered to their door for fifteen cents a week.

If someone wanted it, I had to tell the customer that I would deliver it on Wednesdays and collect the money for it when I gave her the magazine.

I spent two days covering all of Stump City, down County Line Road, and Skaneateles Falls. It took me that long because most of the time a woman would come to the door, and most women have more to say than most men.

I ended up with twenty-four customers. That would give me $1.20 in profits every week. That was a very good, steady income!

I sent the form back in with the number of copies I needed and waited two weeks for the magazines to come.

A decent sized package came on a Tuesday. It was too big to fit into our mailbox, so Mr. Jackson handed it over the counter to me. I quickly thanked him and hurried on home.

When I opened the package, I was surprised to see a carrying sack with <u>TV Guide</u> printed on one side. I counted the magazines and they had given me one extra.

I anxiously waited for Wednesday to come. It took a long time to deliver all the magazines because the route covered a big area. Most of the customers were home and were happy to see me. Some people gave me a tip of a penny or two and a few gave me a nickel.

When I got home I counted up the money, checked it with the list I carried, and sent $2.40 to headquarters. I had to take some money out of what I got in tips to cover those customers who weren't home, but I knew the people who hadn't paid would be good for it.

Over the next month or so, I gained seven new customers because some of those who had said no when I first went around had changed their minds.

It was good to be in business for myself. Once in awhile I even gave Mom some of the money to help pay for household expenses.

ALMOST A HEART ATTACK DUMMY

Soaping windows was still fun on Halloween and the candy was good, but I was looking for more excitement. I soon found out that Davey and Pete could supply it for me.

Instead of going around with kids from house to house for the whole night, I just wanted to go long enough to get a few days supply of candy and soap some windows. I got Mrs. Morton's house really good! It only took an hour or so out of the night to get candy and do the soaping.

I carried my candy bag back home and wandered back up to Stump Road to see what else was going on. I found Davey and Pete in the Walton yard. They were stuffing a well-worn flannel shirt and a ratty looking pair of pants with leaves. When they saw me coming, they just looked at me and smiled in a fashion indicating they were up to no good.

Without saying anything, I got an arm full of leaves and started helping them. It didn't take very long to finish the job because the maple trees had dropped lots of leaves and the winds hadn't yet been strong enough to blow them away. The stuffing done, Davey tied some bailing twine around the waist of the dummy to hold the two halves together. We were stumped on what to do for a head until Davey came up with the idea of using a burlap feed bag. He ran to his barn and got one. We quickly stuffed it. It looked something like a head with a few lumps in odd places. Another piece of twine was used to tie it to the shirt.

We stood there looking down at the dummy, not saying a word as we admired our handy work.

I broke the silence by asking, "What are we going to do with it?

It became obvious that neither Davey nor Pete had thought that far ahead.

Silence again.

The silence was broken by a car passing. This didn't happen very often because Stump Road wasn't well traveled unless someone was going to or from Auburn. All the stores in Auburn were closed for a good two hours by this time, so the traffic was very light.

"I have it!" Pete said it as if he had come up with the cure for some bad disease.

"You have what?" Davey said not catching on to what was going on in Pete's head.

"We can put a pile of leaves in the middle of the road and stick the dummy in it."

Of course, Davey and I thought Pete had come up with a great idea.

We all gathered leaves in our arms. In no time we had a decent pile in the road.

Davey got the dummy and put it in the pile so it had a leg, arm, and its head sticking out.

All excited, we waited. Our ears were listening for the sound of a car and our eyes were looking for lights either coming around the bend and up the road or coming up the hill from the County Line Road direction.

Davey startled me when he said, "Why don't we tie a rope around the dummy's head, and throw the end of the rope over the tree limb that's right above the road?"

"What good is that going to do?" Pete asked.

"Don't you see? Davey said and continued when neither of us answered, "We can yank the dummy out of the pile just as a car gets close."

Pete and I thought Davey had come up with something close to being brilliant.

"I'll get a rope and the ladder," Davey said as he hustled off towards the barn.

It didn't take long for us to tie the rope around the dummy's neck and get the rope over the big branch.

Since Davey had come up with the idea, he would be the one to yank the dummy out of the leaves when a car came.

Pete and I decided that we should hide in a different spot because the tree wasn't big enough for all three of us to hide behind.

We were getting tired of waiting but determined to see the fruits of our labors. Kids were walking from house to house in their costumes. When one went over to see what was in the road, he jumped as Davey gave the rope a short yank which rustled the leaves and moved the dummy's head a bit. It was dark enough to give them a good scare.

Some of the kids were tired of walking and little by little we had a crowd scattered around the area waiting for a car to come by. I noticed my little sister Pat squatting down in the field across the street with a big Cheshire cat grin on her face. I could also hear Terry talking to Charlotte Walters somewhere further back in the field.

As time passed ever so slowly, I listened to kids chattering here and there. Boredom was setting in.

"There's a car coming!" Some little kid yelled in a high, squeaky voice.

I looked in both directions because it was now too dark to see where he was pointing.

Someone yelled, "Where?"

The spotter yelled, "It's coming up the hill by Walters."

I looked in that direction and saw the faint headlights of a car climbing up the backside of the hill.

"Run for cover!" Davey yelled.

The kids who were standing around talking scattered and hid behind trees, houses, and in the vacant lot across from the Walton home.

I ended up by a tree in front of the Kulle house.

The sedan was coming slowly down the road and getting closer to the dummy. The driver didn't see the pile of leaves until he was almost on top of it. That's when Davy yanked the dummy out of the leaves.

The screeching of the car's brakes and the muffled thud as the front bumper hit the dummy caused mass panic. Kids were running every which-way. I was too!

I half killed myself when I ran full tilt into a low branch and ended up on my back. I ignored the pain and was up and headed for home like a horse galloping for the barn to escape a pack of wolves.

Someone passed me—I think it was Pete. It's a good thing he was in front because he found the chicken wire fence for me. I quickly veered off to the left and took a different route not bothering to look back to see what had happened to him. At this point, it was every man for himself.

I stood on our front porch trying to catch my breath and noticed my sister Pat was already there leaning against a post. We couldn't talk but heard the faint sounds of a man swearing between our hard breathing.

Trying to act normal after such an event wasn't easy, but I gave it my best shot when I went through the kitchen door. Pat stayed on the porch to get her breathing more under control.

"Did you have a good time and stay out of trouble?" Mom said from the living room where she and Dad were watching television.

"We scared some kids and did a few other things," I said in what I thought was my normal tone.

"Were there lots of kids out?" Dad asked.

By this time I was at the kitchen sink filling a glass with water, and Pat was next to me waiting her turn. After a big swallow I said, "They were going everywhere."

This was a fact and not even close to a lie, but, again, I knew I wasn't being totally honest.

Dad chuckled and said, "I remember the time we got caught tipping over Old Man Mitchell's outhouse with him in it."

"Vinnie!" Mom said.

"Ethel, we didn't know he was in it until we heard him yelling and cussing. By then it was too late. The outhouse had reached the point of no return. We scattered like hens from a fox."

"Did you get caught?" I asked as I entered the living room. It never dawned on me that Dad would think about doing something like that.

"No, but I was sure scared I would for a good week after."

Just then we heard a knock at the door.

"It's too late for trick or treating," Dad said as he got up from his lumpy sofa chair.

"Why, Mr. Walton, what brings you here at this time of night?" Dad said.

"Good evening, John. Mr. McLaughlin came to my door just a few minutes ago. He was white as a ghost and holding onto his chest. He thought he had run over someone in front of our house. I went back outside with him expecting to find some child dead in the road. It was only a dummy." Mr. Walton said all this with great seriousness.

"Sounds like a prank gone bad, Dave. Is Mr. McLaughlin all right?"

Mr. Walton answered, "Yes, Vinnie. When he saw it was only a dummy, he went wild with cussing, got back into his car, and left." He continued, "Davy said that he, Pete, and Michael were the ones who did it."

"Is that so." Dad said. "I'll talk to Michael about it."

"Thanks, John."

Dad closed the door behind Mr. Walton and returned to the living room, sat down, and was silent for a few moments.

"Michael, I know you were just trying to have some fun. Before you do something like that again, try to think first."

"I'm sorry, Dad. I won't try something like that again." I said and waited for Dad to stand up and pull his belt off.

Mom was expecting it too.

Dad just sat there watching the television. Finally, he said, "It's getting awfully late. You'd better get yourself ready for bed."

I did as I was told and got into bed quickly before Dad changed his mind about the belt.

I lay there thinking about the night and the great fun we'd had—up till the point of the car hitting the dummy.

Just before I went to sleep, I made a connection between dummies and outhouses and knew why Dad's belt had stayed in its loops.

GRAVITY WORKS

When I got off the bus I always waved to Mr. Hanville and beat feet for home. If Mom needed something done, I did it quickly and got myself headed up the road to find someone to play with.

Long ago Mom gave up pestering me about school work and was just happy at the end of each school year if I passed into the next grade, so homework wasn't an issue.

If I got past the Walton house because Davey was busy or not there, I always saw the Kulle boys sitting at their dining room table doing their school work as I walked towards Pete's house. Mrs. Kulle put a high price on learning. This probably explains why the boys always got good grades.

I didn't get to play with Bobby and Dick Kulle much because their Mom seemed to have them on a regular schedule for homework, housework, and outdoor chores.

On Saturdays Bobby and Dick were cut free to play after they finished feeding the chickens and cleaning up the droppings, but I didn't go to their house much.

I was afraid of Mrs. Kulle. Heck, she might put me to work or sit me down at the dining room table to catch up on my school work, which would take at least a week.

One Saturday afternoon, for some unknown reason, the two boys ended up at our kitchen door asking Mom if I could come out and play.

We went to the backyard to goof around. One of them got the idea of going to the community quarry dump behind our place to check it out. They had never been allowed to go there and were curious to find out what they were missing.

After looking to make sure Pal wasn't grazing in the area, we quickly ran to the rim of the quarry.

"That sure is a long way down," Bobby said while peering over the edge.

"Mike, is there a place where we can climb down and not get all cut up?" Dick asked.

"Yeah, it's up a little further. Follow me."

I led them to the only spot where I could pretend I was a mountain climber without killing myself. It was still scary enough because the loose stones and dirt always caused me to slip some on the way up or down the cliff.

Dick said, "Let's try it."

I went first to show them the zigzag way I climbed down. I stopped and yelled back up when I got to a spot that caused me problems in other climbs and said things like: "Look out for this spot, there's a sharp rock with moss on it. There's a slippery root here. Don't step on it."

Because I was concentrating so much on giving them instructions, I almost lost my footing on a stone when I lowered myself down from one ledge to another.

Safely at the bottom, I yelled back up, "Who's next?"

Dick said, "I'll go."

Dick came down without any problems, and Bobby started just as soon as Dick was standing next to me.

We watched him quickly come down, probably because he wanted to show up his older brother.

Bobby gave his brother a very cocky grin and said, "What next?"

I pointed to the little hills covered with small trees in the quarry and said, "It's fun to climb up and down them."

It was a hot day and we began to sweat from all the running around. After we conquered all the hills in the quarry and were standing at the top of the last one, we were all pooped out.

When we caught our breaths, we decided to head on back to my house for water.

"Do you want to take the easy way out, or climb back up the cliff?" I asked.

Bobby said, "I want to go up the cliff."

"Okay," I said.

Dick wanted to go first. He went up as fast as he could to prove to his younger brother that he was still stronger and faster. Not to be outdone, Bobby tried to go faster.

I watched him going up with my head slowly going backward as he got higher. He was moving too quickly. I could tell that being cautious wasn't on his mind. Just before he got to the top, he stood on a small ledge and reached for a stone to pull himself up. As he grabbed it, the stone came free and Bobby went backwards with his arms working like the wings of a crazy bird.

I had to jump to one side because he was coming down in my area, so I didn't see how he landed. I did hear a dull thud as he hit.

In a state of shock I said, "Bobby, are you okay?"

He got up slowly, crying and holding his forehead.

Dick was now down the cliff and looking at Bobby.

"You're bleeding!" Dick said in a high pitched tone.

Bobby pulled his hand away from his head and nearly passed out when he saw the blood. His crying instantly got louder.

Dick looked at me with big eyes and said, "We've got to get him home."

We walked on either side of Bobby, propping him up as much as we could. This time we were taking the easy way out of the quarry.

Mom heard Bobby's wailing as we got closer to the house. She knew the difference between crying for nothing and crying in pain and was quickly running up the hill to meet us.

Mom yelled, "What happened?"

"Bobby fell down the quarry," I yelled back.

After carefully examining Bobby's wound, Mom turned to Dick and said, "Go home and get your mother. Run!"

Dick took off like a shot while Mom and I half carried Bobby into the house.

"We'll bring him into the living room and put him on the couch."

We gently lowered him onto the couch and Mom put a pillow under Bobby's bleeding head.

"Stay with him, Michael. I'm going to get a damp towel."

By the time she got back, Bobby's blood had coated the pillow and was dripping onto the sheet covering the holes in our old couch.

Mom knelt on the floor and pressed the towel onto the wound.

She calmed Bobby down by saying, "There, there, Bobby, you'll be all right."

The kitchen door burst open. Mrs. Kulle came charging in yelling, "Bobby, Bobby!" When she saw all the blood, she went into a panic mode, which set Bobby off again. He started to cry loudly.

Everything became a blur. Mr. Kulle came next. He picked Bobby up and carried him home with his wife at his side trying to comfort Bobby as they trotted up the street.

To take her mind off of what had just happened, Mom said, "I've got to wash all the bloody things before the blood sets."

I helped her gather up the blood covered things. Once down in the cellar, Mom fired up the Maytag washing machine.

When everything was in the machine and going around and around, Mom looked directly into my eyes and said, "What happened, Michael?"

I told her everything and made the mistake of adding, "I've never had a problem climbing there before."

"This isn't the first time you've been climbing in the dump! I thought you had more sense than to do something like that!" She said this with disbelief in her voice and concluded with, "Wait til your father hears about this!"

When Dad heard, his belt came off and I got a good dose of the usual.

Later that night, we found out Bobby had to be taken to the hospital to be examined and got a load of stitches.

Every time I saw Bobby after the stitches came out, I was reminded of what happened at the quarry because he had a beautiful white scar on his forehead.

THE BLIND TEACHING THE BLIND

Around the time Bobby fell, I had a good, established <u>TV Guide</u> route. The only things that slowed me down when I delivered them were deep snow, mean dogs, and chatty customers. I made a game out of seeing how fast I could cover the route. I checked the time on my Roy Roger's watch as I left our porch and checked it again when I got back onto the porch with an empty sack. If all conditions seemed to be good, I pushed myself extra hard and tried to break my record delivery time.

Off and on I heard Mom talking to Mrs. Tambroni about a little boy who lived next door to the Tambroni place on Jordan Road, but I had never seen him when I passed his house delivering magazines. His name was Joey O'Hara. From what I could gather without being a complete eavesdropper, Joey was around my sister Pat's age, had gone totally blind, and didn't go to school.

I didn't know any other blind person except ancient Mrs. Moony and was curious about Joey because he was only four or five years younger than me. I also had an overactive imagination and began to imagine myself becoming blind. I scared myself by thinking about walking around with a cane and falling or tripping over things all the time while I was trying to play like a regular kid.

Walking up the slight grade on Jordan Road and just a few houses past Mr. Seguin's garage, I finally spotted Joey O'Hara sitting on the front porch all bundled up in a blanket and staring out toward the road. His head was bigger than normal and his dark, penetrating eyes seemed to be sunken in some.

I got the strangest feeling that he was staring at me, so I said, "Hi, Joey. It's Mike Quigley. How are you doing today?

"Hi, Mike. Isn't it a beautiful day?" He said with a big smile on his face.

"Sure is. I'm delivering the TV Guide, or I'd stop and talk to you," I said.

Saying it without even thinking, I added, "I come by your house every Wednesday about this time."

"See ya, Mike," Joey said in my direction with a high wave of an arm he pulled out from under the blanket.

I thought about Joey on and off while walking the rest of my route. How could anyone act so cheerful when he was blind and stuck on a porch?

By the time the next Wednesday rolled around, I had forgotten about Joey O'Hara. All the conditions were perfect for a record run on my route, and I was ahead of schedule by the time I began chugging up the slight grade by Joey's house.

Concentrating so much on keeping up a fast pace, I was startled when I heard a voice say, "Hi, Mike. Sure is a beautiful day."

It was Joey. How did he hear me coming? I wasn't a heavy walker and I was on a paved road. Come to think of it, how did he know it was me?

I said, "Hi, Joey. It sure is. How are you doing today?"

"I'm just fine," he said with a smile.

For some reason I was drawn to Joey, so I walked up to the porch and began to talk to him. We chitchatted like boys do for a few minutes until we both ran out of words.

I finally said, "Well, I have to get going now. I'll see you next week."

"Okay, Mike. It was fun talking to you. Thanks for stopping," He said this in a tone that told me he indeed did have a good time with me.

After a few more deliveries, I realized that my record wouldn't be broken on the run, so I slowed my pace down.

As long as the weather was halfway decent, Joey was sitting on the porch. We began to play an unspoken game with me trying to be extra quiet with my footsteps to see how close to his house I could get before he said, "Hi, Mike."

Joey was better at it than I was, because he said his "Hi, Mike" with an extra large grin on his face much before I got in front of his house.

I looked forward to our short conversations and knew Joey did too. We always talked about our families, the weather, and what we had done in the past week.

It was a perfect day for delivering the magazine, so I was very surprised to not see Joey sitting on the front porch. Did he have to go someplace with his Mom?

Joey wasn't on the porch the next Wednesday either.

I decided to ask Mom about Joey when I got home.

"Mom, where's Joey O'Hara? I haven't seen him on his front porch for over two weeks."

"Poor Joey. He's taken a turn for the worse and now must stay in bed." Mom sighed and said with sadness in her voice.

She continued, "I don't know what's going on around here. Your cousin, Elizabeth Major, has a tumor on her brain too and she is blind."

I noticed Mom was shaking her head in a thoughtful way when she continued as if talking to herself, "The way polio hit people a few years ago has me wondering if it's some new type of disease we have to worry about."

When she saw the scared look on my face, she knew she should have kept that thought to herself.

"Don't worry, Michael. Of course it isn't a disease. Why, we would have heard about it in the newspaper if it was." She tried to say in a reassuring voice.

I breathed a little easier and said, "Will Joey be okay, Mom?"

"He's very sick, Michael. I don't think so. It would be a good idea to pray for him."

I prayed for Joey every night before I went to sleep and thought about him the next two times I went by his house.

One afternoon Mom said in a sad, quiet voice, "Come here, Michael. I want to talk to you."

I knew something was wrong and just stood in front of her with my hands down by my sides.

"Michael, little Joey O'Hara is dead."

After what she said registered in my head, I started to cry. Mom held me close saying, "There, there, Michael. It's for the best."

I said to myself, "For the best! For the best for who? Not Joey or me!"

Joey and I had become friends. He never mentioned being blind and I never brought it up because it didn't matter.

Just because he couldn't run and play like me didn't mean he couldn't be happy.

LIKE SHOOTING FISH IN A BARREL

Late spring finally arrived. I say "finally" because the time after winter and during the early spring wasn't the greatest. One day it would be nice and warm and the next snow would be on the ground. It would melt and everything would be muddy. It was almost impossible to play on lawns, so we were limited to the streets.

I happened to be out front picking up stones from the side of the road and pretending that some branch or tree trunk was an enemy. If I hit my target, I'd say, "Got ya, you lousy vermin."

I was concentrating on the next enemy to kill, a branch in a tree, when a loud gunshot went off close by. It threw my aim off by at least five feet, and the loud bang brought me back to the real world in a jiffy.

I stood still looking in the direction I heard the shot coming from waiting for another. A minute or so later it came again and echoed off the back wall of Welch Allyn. Someone was shooting a .22 down by the bridge on Stump Road.

I hustled up our road and down to the bridge. Davey, Pete, and Dick O'Hara were watching Dick's brother, Don, aiming his rifle at the water. I came up on them without saying a word and looked into the water.

There had to be a dozen or so huge fish swimming close to the surface. When one slowly came up to the top, I could tell it was a trout. Its gills were working hard, and it looked like it didn't have long to live.

The gun went off with a loud crack. The fish suddenly came to life and went under. A few seconds later, it came to the surface again, but this time it was dead. I noticed two other dead trout slowly floating down towards the mill dam.

"Let me have a shot," Dick said.

Don handed over the rifle to him.

Dick took his turn. Another trout went under and came back up dead.

This went on until all the trout I could see were floating toward the dam.

None of us said anything to the O'Hara boys.

I know I didn't want to because I was too scared to say anything. Davey and Pete probably felt the same way.

We three left the O'Hara boys and walked back up the road.

Davey said, "Have you ever seen bigger fish?"

Pete said, "No. They must have come over the dam at Skaneateles when the water was high."

"I'm surprised that they lived to make it this far with all the garbage in the water," Davey said.

I nodded in agreement because I once put my hand in the water and had to quickly pull it out. The colored water seemed to burn and left my hand red and itchy even after I washed it when I got home.

The beautiful fish never stood a chance after they left their home in the pure waters of Skaneateles Lake.

CHOPPING MORE THAN WEEDS

Not long after Dad surprised my sister, Terry, by bringing home a horse, Rocky, he decided that it was time to take back the whole field behind the house for Rocky's eating pleasure. Mr. O'Hara came and removed his fencing from the field, and Dad staked Rocky out with a chain attached to his halter. The stake was moved a few times a week because Rocky ate the grass down in a neat circle making it too short for him to chew up a decent meal.

When Dad saved enough money to buy electric fence wiring and an electric weed chopper, I helped him string the fencing on the fence posts Mr. O'Hara left behind. After we were through stringing the wire around white insulators Dad attached to each pole, I watched him mount the weed chopper box to the wall inside the shed. It had a cord with a plug connected to an outlet and a wire he connected from the box to a feed line running to the fence. When it was turned on, it sent a powerful pulse of electricity through the feed wire and around the fenced-in field. I could hear the weed chopper making a clicking sound every two or three seconds telling us the juice was shooting out of the box and through the fence.

Dad decided that the system was working properly, and I followed him out of the barn and up to the fencing.

"Son, there are two ways of checking to see if there is a current going through the fencing. You can use this fence tester," he said as he pulled it out of his pocket.

I looked at it. It had a black rubber top with a little light bulb in it and a short, hard rubber handle to hold. A cord dangled down from the top piece and had a metal prong attached to its end.

Dad said as he demonstrated, "Let me show you how it works. First, you put the prong into the ground close to the fence. Next, you put the bulb end against the fence where you see the bare metal. If the light comes on, you know you have juice going through the line."

"Now, it's your turn to try," he said as he took the bulb end off the fence and pulled the prong out of the ground.

I did it the way he showed me. The little light glowed and went out just like it did when Dad put the tester onto the fence

"Good. Oh, there's one other thing. Make sure to put the prong in the ground first so you don't get a shock."

"Dad, what's the other way to test the fence?"

"You take the back of your hand and put it on the under side of the fence like this."

I heard a sparking noise as Dad touched the fence. His hand went down real fast.

"It sure packs a punch!" Dad said. "No wonder it's called a weed chopper. There's enough juice in it to chop off any weeds that grow up to it."

"Why did you use the back of your hand and not just grab onto it?" I asked.

"If you grab it, your fingers might contract because of the shock and you might have a heck of a time getting your hand free."

"Do you want to do it?" He added.

I was scared but decided I'd give it a try.

I slowly raised the back of my hand up towards the wire. I got a jolt that threw my hand down and vibrated my whole body at the same time.

Dad laughed as I jumped up and down for a few seconds.

"By the way, don't try that when the grass is wet. You'd get even a bigger shock."

"Don't worry. I won't." I said with complete sincerity.

"Now, go get the gang from the house. I want them to see how Rocky reacts to being freed."

"Okay," I said as I turned towards the house.

Dad waited until we were all out by the fence to release Rocky from his chain.

Rocky went charging around the fenced-in area enjoying his freedom. He was having a grand old time. He finally took a breather and walked up to the fence on the McEneny side. He got close to sniff it and almost went straight up into the air. Rocky quickly turned and ran away kicking his rear heels in the air.

"It works," Dad said in a dry way.

We all laughed.

We watched Rocky explore other areas of the fence. He came away from them in a big hurry when he got shocked.

It didn't take him long to realize that his freedom had boundaries, and he stayed away from the fencing. However, within a few weeks, Rocky was testing his boundaries and carefully sticking his head under the fencing to reach greener grass. He got good at it but got jolted enough times to keep from getting too cocky.

Rocky and I were much alike.

The O'Reilly family lived on School Street a few houses up from Jordan Road. I knew they had a boy around my age, but I didn't play with him. He went to Skaneateles School, so he might as well have lived twenty miles away. It was very hard to get to know kids who went to a different school.

Mom must have talked to Mrs. O'Reilly about having her son, Kevin, over to our house to play because Mom told me that he would be coming over soon.

I had heard about Kevin being a troublemaker and a spoiled brat but never experienced his ways myself. I wasn't anxious to play with him.

When Kevin came over, Mom greeted him and called to me. "Michael, Kevin is here to play."

I came in the back door and said, "Hi, Kevin, what do you want to do?"

Kevin had dark hair, a few freckles on his face, a skinny body, and huge ears. He reminded me of Alfalfa on the <u>Little Rascal Show</u>.

He said in a sullen tone, "I don't know."

"Why don't we go outside and play in my tree fort?" I said in a fake, cheerful manner.

I went out with Kevin shuffling slowly behind me. I pointed out the fort in the apple tree I spent many hours putting together with old boards and used nails on the flat "Y" part of a huge branch. It was only big enough for two to sit on and didn't have any walls, but I had built it all by myself and took pride in my workmanship.

"That's a tree fort?" Kevin said and continued, "Why, that's just a piece of junk."

I could tell that we weren't getting off on the right foot.

"I think it's grand." I retorted.

Kevin came back with, "It stinks. Mine is much nicer. My brother helped me build it."

He then took notice of small, green apples on the ground and picked one up. He smiled as he pegged one right at me.

I ducked just in time. "Hey, why did you do that?"

"Can't take it, huh?. He paused and continued, "What do you want to do?"

"Let's go up by the fence and call Rocky." I said.

Who's Rocky?"

He's my sister, Terry's, horse." Turning away from him I yelled, "Rocky, come here, boy."

Just as Rocky was getting close to us, Kevin pegged an apple at him. It hit his leg and Rocky took off across the field in a trot.

"What do you think you're doing?" I yelled.

Kevin just laughed and said, "No big deal. Hey, I've got to go pee."

Without thinking I said, "Bet you can't hit the fence."

"That's an easy shot," he said.

Before I knew it, he hit the fence with his water and flew backwards from it like he had a rope attached to his belt and was being pulled by a speeding car. He landed on his back, rolled a few times, bounced to his feet and started running towards home howling like a wounded cat.

I stood there watching and listening to him as he quickly faded up our road. I almost felt sorry for what I had done to him.

When I went back into the house, Mom said, "Where's Kevin?"

"Oh, he wanted to go home. He didn't have much fun here."

"He didn't stay very long. Maybe he will come back another day." She said.

I was worried that Mrs. O'Reilly would tell Mom what happened, but she never did. I figured that Kevin was too embarrassed to tell her about it.

Dad sure was right about not mixing water with electricity.

BOY SCOUTS AND DOUGHNUTS

When I became too old to be in Cub Scouts in Elbridge anymore, I joined the Boy Scout troop in Skaneateles Falls. Meetings were held once a week in the basement of the American Legion. Years earlier the boys and their leaders had made the cellar look almost presentable by painting the walls and putting in tables and chairs. Boy Scout posters were taped to the walls showing camping scenes, different knots we had to learn, and a well-scrubbed Boy Scout giving the proper hand salute.

I couldn't afford a complete uniform and had to make due with a used shirt, neckerchief, and yellow neckerchief slide. Only one boy in our troop had the complete uniform, including the hat.

We had fun learning how to tie different knots, how to build a fire without using gasoline, pitching a tent so a slight breeze wouldn't blow it over, cooking food, and the Boy Scout Oath.

Hub Cashin, Pete's much older brother, was the Scout Master and Pee Wee Wright was his assistant. Pee Wee got his name because of his size. He was even shorter than me!

Meetings were held during the school week after supper time and lasted for about an hour. I had a good time at the meetings until it was about time for them to end. Then I started to think about walking home in the dark and missed part of what was being taught or said because of it.

It was real scary going down by the creek because Marty, the town drunk, sometimes would drink under the bridge and fall asleep. Once, as I was just crossing the middle of the bridge, he moaned in a most eerie way. I swear, I didn't feel my feet touching the ground until they hit the steps of our kitchen porch.

I got all excited about my first camping trip and had all the required gear ready to go the night before the venture.

Right after school on a Friday, we all met at the Legion. We loaded all the tents, firewood, food and other gear into the back of a pickup truck and took off for a camping spot a few miles down on Stump Road.

The two most junior in the troop—I was one of them - were assigned the job of digging a latrine. We found a spot just far and downwind enough from the camping area to keep unpleasant smells away from it. It wasn't easy because the spot also had to have a good sapling to lean back on. It took us a long time to dig a hole two feet deep. Not long after it passed Mr. Cashin's inspection, it was put to use.

We had the campsite all set up long before dark and a good fire was burning with food cooking in frying pans.

After we ate and got all the cooking gear washed up, we built the fire up and sat around it listening to Pee Wee tell stories. The scariest one he told was about a huge, toothless man who roamed in the very woods we were camping looking for kids who hadn't been good.

Just as he finished, Davy touched me on my shoulder and gave me a huge start. Everyone got a good laugh at my expense.

It was getting late, so Mr. Cashin had us get into our assigned tents. I curled up under my two blankets, ignored the stone sticking into my side, and was soon asleep.

Around two in the morning, I woke up screaming and yelling. I was having a terrible nightmare about a huge man chasing after me.

Everyone in camp woke up. They were all upset that I had disturbed their sleep and let me know about it.

I couldn't get myself settled back down, so Mr. Cashin had to drive me home.

Dad answered the knock on the door and listened while Mr. Cashin explained what had happened while I stood there all embarrassed about my unmanly display of behavior.

Dad said, "I'm sorry this happened, Hub. Maybe he'll do better the next time."

I sure was upset for many weeks about what happened and had a heck of time facing the guys when I saw them on the street and at the next several meetings.

It didn't get better the next time we went camping because the same thing happened again. This time Dad came along to help out, so he ended up taking me home.

Nothing was said in the car, but I was very agitated with myself that it had happened.

From then on, I didn't go on any camping trips. I stayed home while the rest of the troop went. From what the boys told me, I sure missed some good times.

It was towards the end of a meeting several months after I gave up camping and I was thinking about the walk across the bridge. As usual, I missed most of what Hub was telling us. All I caught was, "Go around the neighborhood and sell doughnuts." and "We'll meet here next Saturday afternoon at one."

I left the meeting and crossed the bridge without getting mashed by a monster and didn't think anymore about the meeting until Saturday rolled around.

I showed up wearing my Boy Scout shirt, neckerchief, and yellow slide.

"Okay, boys. Listen up. You all know what to do. Take ten boxes of doughnuts each and get started." Mr. Cashin said and continued, "Remember, the money we make will be used to buy new tents and gear."

I got my ten boxes and took off to Stump City and sold them in no time. I went back and asked for more and was off again. Before the afternoon was over, I had sold sixty-two boxes of doughnuts.

After I sold all the boxes I had, I walked back to the Legion and waited for the rest of the troop to slowly trickle back in.

Once we were all there, Mr. Cashin quieted us down and said, "Great job, boys. You sold all of the doughnuts. Now we can get some new equipment."

We all cheered at his words except for one Scout who didn't look very happy.

Mr. Cashin noticed him and asked, "What's the problem, Jim?"

Jim said, "Somebody was selling doughnuts to the homes you told me to go to."

Another boy chimed in, "Yeah, that happened to me too."

Before the chorus was done, two more boys piped up about their territories being invaded by another Scout.

Since a Boy Scout has to be honest, I said, "It must have been me. I'm sorry. I didn't know we were supposed to just sell at certain homes."

Before the boys could jump all over me, Mr. Cashin said, "That's okay, Mike. The important thing is we sold all of them."

I think Mr. Cashin was taking pity on me because I was the youngest in the troop. Besides, he didn't want me to get beaten up after the meeting.

After a pause, one of the kids said, "Mr. Cashin, how are you going to give out the prizes to the three best sellers?"

Prizes? I didn't know there were prizes.

"Well," he said and paused for a moment, "I think Mike should get the top prize."

This didn't sit well with the kid who sold the most without going into other territories, but he kept his mouth shut.

Mr. Cashin handed me a beautiful Boy Scout pocket knife and the boy who came in second a new neckerchief with a yellow neckerchief slide.

On the way out I offered to trade with the boy. He said, Naw, I have a knife but I need a new neckerchief and slide."

I liked the knife but always thought about the way I had won it whenever I took it out to cut something. The thought sure took the edge off that knife.

UNFRIENDLY FIRE

The sudden, shocking move of the Walton family to Arizona made it very quiet around Stump City until their sudden, joyful return about a year later. The "For Sale" sign came down in front of their house, and the noise level went back up to what it had been before they moved.

It was during that time I found out that Santa wasn't real after I pulled down a Daisy Red Rider B.B. gun from the cellar rafters. I became a very good shot with it and honed my skills to the point that I could hit an insect from a good twenty feet. The gun also took most of the sting away from learning that Santa wasn't real.

Davey and I were shooting at tin cans we had set up in his backyard and enjoying the sound as a can took a solid hit. Bobby and Dick Kulle saw us from their backyard, got their B.B. guns and soon joined us in the target practice.

After we had dented the cans in many spots, Dick said, "Hey! How about having a B.B. gun fight?"

The other two were all for it, but I held back. I had promised Dad not to shoot at anyone with it and I intended to keep my promise. Besides, Dad told me he'd take the gun away from me if I did shoot at someone.

"What are you afraid of Mike?" Bobby said with a solid note of sarcasm in his voice.

"Nothing. I just don't want to do it," I said.

"Suit yourself," Davey said.

I stood by the corner of the horse barn the older Walton boys and Mr. Walton had recently built while the boys scattered to get out of each other's range.

All three took cover behind trees, bushes, and buildings. Their shots were hitting everything but live targets. It was easy to tell by the way they acted and talked that they were getting very frustrated with their poor shooting.

I was leaning against the barn with my gun down by my side with a smug grin on my face as I watched their poor shooting. My stance and smirk might have made me look like Wyatt Earp watching a bunch of greenhorns shooting at each other.

Dick happened to glance in my direction and noticed my stance and look. Apparently it didn't sit well with him, so he aimed in my direction. I didn't react fast enough and before I could get myself around the barn corner, I felt a sharp sting in my butt. I didn't drop my precious gun while I jumped up and down rubbing my cheek, but I came close.

Dick was out in the open laughing up a storm when he got nailed in the face by one of the other two. He dropped his gun and started rubbing his chin while he did a good imitation of an Indian doing a war dance.

Davey and Bobby came to their senses when they saw us both hopping around. Maybe they remembered their mothers or fathers saying, "Be careful or I'll..."

The Gunfight at the Walton Lawn came to a quick end, and we all went home without saying much.

When their mother found out what they had been up to, Bobby and Dick had their guns taken away from them for a long time. By some miracle, Davey's Mom and Dad didn't find out, so he was spared.

It's a good thing I loved having my B.B. gun so much that I didn't give in and join the gunfight. I know Mom would have taken it away from me until I was old enough to drive.

BEAVER MEADOW: PART III

I continued to explore Beaver Meadow while avoiding the bull. I learned to look for flashes of white and now knew the difference between a bull and a heifer besides their sizes.

Hunting frogs was fun, but the fun and challenge wore off once I learned the knack of catching them with ease.

The most fun I had while playing by myself in the meadow was pretending to be a cowboy or pioneer on some dangerous mission. The mission would change and grow as I made my way through that wonderful make-believe land.

It was hard to get enough guys together at the same time to have a good cowboy and Indian war in the meadow. I can remember just two times when we had ten or twelve of us playing it.

Right by the fence before entering Beaver Meadow, the two oldest picked teams by playing rock, paper, scissors to see who would be the leader of the cowboy team. Nobody wanted to be the Indian team leader because most of the time the Indians lost on the TV shows or in the movies, so they had to lose when we played.

The cowboy leader chose first. He always picked the boy who was best at sneaking up on others.

Since I was the slowest and youngest, I was picked last both times we played. That meant I was always an Indian and assured of dying many times over before we all got too tired to play the game any longer.

The cowboys used their pointer fingers as gun barrels and their thumbs as gun hammers. The Indians drew back their pretend bows and let arrows fly.

We Indians got a head start, so we could find places to hide and set up ambushes. The cowboys waited a few minutes before they started hunting us down.

The best part of playing this game was finding a good hiding spot where I could jump out and let an arrow fly before the cowboy enemy saw me. I'd yell, "Got ya!" The cowboy had to fall down and pretend he was dead with his eyes closed while I made a quick exit.

What always did us Indians in was the six shooter's accuracy. Its range was a good five times further than a bow and arrow. The cowboys always shot an Indian no matter how far away he was and no matter how much the Indian zigzagged. The cowboys were very cocky and considered themselves to be the best shots in the West, just like the heroes in the movies and TV shows.

We were playing cowboys and Indians in Beaver Meadow on a late, warm spring day for at least an hour and having a great battle in an area by a big swimming hole. With all the Indians dead or dying at the same time, the game became officially over and the cowboys celebrated their victory by shooting their guns into the air.

All of us quieted down and stood by the hole. Sweat was dripping down our faces as we looked at the inviting water thinking about how great it would be to just jump into the cold, spring water. Pete was the first to go into action and started taking off clothes. The rest of us quickly followed his lead.

Before long, we were all jumping into the very cold water and having a great time. The clear water soon became muddy, but we didn't care. Those who could did cannonballs that made a thudding noise with a huge spray of water shooting straight up in the air. Those of us who couldn't, kept practicing without much success. We were all making enough noise to wake the dead.

Happening to turn Pete's way, I noticed him standing still in the water with his ear cocked to one side like a hound dog listening for a possible meal.

"Be quiet!" he whispered loudly.

We noticed the concentration on his face and we all went still.

A boy standing in the water close to Pete said, "Someone is coming!"

We scrambled out of the water as if a huge crocodile had shown up to devour all of us and started putting on our clothes. It was tough going because clothes don't go on quickly over wet bodies.

I had just got on my underpants and was zipping up my dungarees when a couple of the Walton girls and their friends came around a big clump of bushes. They all screamed at the same time, but didn't turn their heads away very quickly.

I felt my face redden to have a bunch of girls catch me like this but felt better when I looked around to see two boys who had foolishly decided to put their shirts on first. They were squatting down holding their shirt-tails against their knees and facing the girls. Their white butts were facing in our direction in a purely accidental mooning position.

One of the girls started to scream even louder, so the rest of them joined in. They all turned and ran from the area as if they had just witnessed a baby being boiled in oil.

As if on cue, we all hurriedly finished dressing and got ourselves out of there.

I don't know why we were in such a big hurry. The damage had been done. Maybe we figured that if it happened from one direction, it could happen from another one.

It's never good to leave your rear flank exposed to the enemy.

The girls who caught us in our almost "all-together" never did say anything to us about the encounter, but I was embarrassed for the longest time and knew my face turned bright red whenever I ran into one of the girls I saw at the swimming hole.

COURTS AND HIGH JUMPING

The Walton's main barn was very close to the edge of Stump Road. It wasn't all that big, but we had fun playing in it. When the hay supply got low in the back part of the barn, Johnny, an older Walton boy, and Davey put a piece of plywood up on one of the walls and attached a well-used basketball hoop without a net to it.

There wasn't room for more than four guys to play at a time, and the walls were declared out of bounds. Sometimes going out of bounds was very painful, especially if I got help from one of the boys. Davey found a hammer and flattened the sharp ends of the nails sticking through the barn siding to stop further punctures into our various body parts. The rules were pretty loose and a player had to be hurt before a foul was called.

The indoor basketball season depended on the amount of hay in the barn and the weather. Once the good weather came, we played outside on a plywood backboard held up by two rickety poles. There was no grass growing on the court because it had all been worn off. If the ground was wet, the court was like a skating ring. An old towel was kept just off the court to wipe the mud off the ball.

One winter we had a huge amount of snow on the ground and the town snowplow made a high snow bank in front of the barn.

Someone, it might have been Davey, came up with the idea of jumping out of the hayloft through the open door and into the pile of snow. I watched Pete go first just to see if he survived the leap. When he hit, he buried himself almost up to his waist in the snow but hadn't come close to reaching the frozen ground beneath it.

My first jump was the most thrilling. Just getting the nerve up to put my toes over the edge of the doorway, lean over, and push off with my legs to make sure I hit the deep snow was a huge challenge. I hesitated a few seconds and made the leap. I landed feet first and was buried up to my waist. It took me some time to wiggle out.

Several of us jumped more than once, but we got tired of it after the thrill of not knowing if we'd survive the plunge began to fade.

The jumping was put to a halt when one of the younger Walton kids tried it and came up short. He landed just far enough into the deeper snow not to die but get hurt and went yelling into the house. In a matter of seconds, Mrs. Walton came out and told us to stop.

It's probably a good thing that this happened because Pete was talking about jumping out so his butt hit first. The earlier, minor accident probably prevented Pete from taking a trip to the hospital.

BAD SNOWBALL

That same winter a bunch of us boys were wandering around Skaneateles Falls and ended up at the front of Gorham's Garage. The garage was on the corner of Stump and Jordan Road and on the same side of the street as Rodak's Bar. The back of the garage was almost against the hill, and its roof top was just a few feet higher than the part of the hill that was dug out so there'd be room to build the garage.

The left side of the garage was used for repairing cars. The right side had a showroom. The showroom always had a brand new Pontiac on display. Currently, there was a sparkling new two-tone Pontiac Chieftain with chrome bumpers and lots of chrome trim. It sure looked beautiful.

We got tired of looking and talking about it and became silent. It's not a good thing when a group of boys is standing around with nothing to do.

Davey was looking up at the front of the garage and said, "I bet we can go around back and get on the roof."

I have to admit that I thought about doing the very same thing months earlier. At the time I was by myself and decided it wasn't a good idea. But coming from Davey made it a good idea.

Lots of "Yeah, let's do it!" were said to get up our courage just like a football team gathers around before a game and makes lots of animal noises.

Before I had a chance to get my brain working properly, I was following the gang around to the back of the garage. If we weren't up to something bad, we would have walked back there like normal people, but we walked hunched over a little, which automatically put us up to no good.

I watched the other boys jump onto the flat, garage roof. I leaped without even giving the gap between the bank and the roof a second thought.

Once we were all on board the roof, we started packing snowballs from the snow piled up there. We did this because the snow was there, and we didn't have anything better to do to keep our hands busy. We began aiming at different targets below us to see who could get the closest. One minute it would be the stop sign, the next a telephone pole across the street.

We were quietly playing this game and having fun when a car slowly went by Rodak's Bar and passed in front of the garage. Pete threw a snowball at it and missed. He hadn't figured in the fact that the car was moving, so the snowball landed behind it.

The new game was on! When a car came by, which wasn't very often, we all threw a snowball and ducked down behind the short, front wall. If we got lucky, one or two of the snowballs made a thudding noise as it hit the passing victim. We peeked over the edge to see the cars slow down a bit as the drivers looked to find the source of the enemy fire. None of the drivers figured out where the snowballs were coming from, so we had a grand time feeling safe in our concealed position.

We were all getting good with throwing snowballs ahead of the cars so that they'd drive into the "bombs." If we were lucky, we'd hear "Thud! Thud! Thud! Thud!" This meant an almost perfect round.

The cold, winter air was starting to hit bone level, so we decided to wait for one more "enemy tank" to come by. Naturally, the "enemy" took longer than usual to show up. We occupied our time by really packing our snowballs.

We heard the final "enemy" slowly coming up the road and got into position. Five "thuds" told us that we had all landed fatal blows. We peeked over the edge to see a man getting out of his car looking around for his attackers. He then looked at his windshield and looked around again.

In the dim light given off by the street lamp in front of Rodak's, the man looked slightly familiar.

We all stayed hunkered down behind the wall and were not moving. It seemed like forever until we heard the car door close and the driver continue on.

We peered over the wall to see the car disappearing around the slight bend by the Legion. Then we got up and quickly got off the roof. We talked about the great time we had and split up once we got back to Stump City, each of us heading for home.

After I took off my coat, hat, gloves, and boots in the back room, I went into the kitchen.

Dad was on our almost new phone talking to someone, so I was quiet. I heard the last part of the conversation.

"I'm sorry this had to happen, Mr. Goodrich. Michael and I will come up after I get home from work tomorrow. Good-bye."

Dad hung up the phone and turned to me with anger and disappointment in his eyes. "Michael, what ever possessed you to do such a thing?"

I knew that I was in deep trouble. Once I heard the name "Mr. Goodrich" being spoken on the phone, I instantly put a name to the face I had seen in the dim streetlight.

"We were pretending that the cars were enemy tanks!" I blurted out.

"Well, Mr. Goodrich's tank got a broken windshield!" Dad said.

I didn't know what to say. How could a snowball break a windshield? It then dawned on me about the long wait between cars and how hard we had packed our snowballs.

"I didn't mean any harm, Dad," I said lamely.

"The harm has been done. Mr. Goodrich saw you on the top of Gorham's Garage. We are going to his house tomorrow afternoon right after I get home from work and pay him money for a new windshield."

After a slight pause, Dad added, "And you are going to pay the whole amount back to me!"

"Yes, Dad. I'm really sorry."

"Mr. Goodrich is the one you will be apologizing to tomorrow. Now get yourself up to bed!"

I could tell by the coloring in Dad's face that he had worked himself up pretty good, so I said, "Yes, Sir," and got myself out of the kitchen in a big hurry.

The next day in school was torture. I could only think about facing Mr. Goodrich as I watched the clock slowly tick off the minutes.

When Dad got home from work, he told me to get my coat on and come with him.

It was a very quiet ride up to Mr. Goodrich's house, except for what Dad suggested I say to Mr. Goodrich. Fortunately, he only lived a bit passed Mr. Cronaeur's General Store, so my inner shaking didn't last very long.

It seemed like a long walk up to Mr. Goodrich's trailer. His car was parked close by, so I could see the big crack in the windshield as we walked to his front door.

As we got closer, Mr. Goodrich came out.

"Hello, John," he said in a somber voice.

"Hello, Jim. Michael has something to say to you."

I looked Mr. Goodrich in the eye just as Dad had told me to do and said, "I'm very sorry that I broke your windshield. Dad will pay you the money now, and I will pay him back. I won't be throwing snowballs at cars again."

Mr. Goodrich said, "I'm sorry that this had to happen. I know you weren't the only boy on the roof, but I did see your face and not the others."

Dad handed the money to him and said, "It doesn't matter about the other boys, Jim."

After they said good-bye to each other, Dad and I climbed back into the car.

As Dad pulled back onto Jordan Road he said, "Michael, let this be a lesson to you. You will pay me back the twenty-five dollars it cost for a new windshield."

"Yes, sir."

How was I going to come up with twenty-five dollars? I had saved lots of money the summer before, but spent thirty-five dollars on a new bike. All I had left was around five dollars. I saved that money to buy an ice cream once a week and milk each day to go along with my lunches.

I sure couldn't mow lawns with snow on the ground, and Big Jim McEneny's thirst for Genesee beer faded with the cold weather, so trips to resupply him at Cronaeur's Store were done until the temperature went up.

When we got home, I took all my money out of the jar I kept in the kitchen and gave it to Dad. It came to a little less than five dollars.

I soon figured out a way to make money. I started shoveling sidewalks and driveways around the neighborhood. Many times I thought of Mr. Goodrich's windshield while I shoveled. I continued to think of Mr. Goodrich's windshield once the weather turned and I started mowing lawns again.

It took me until the middle of the summer to pay off my debt to Dad.

None of the other boys ever talked to me about having to pay for the damage. I could sense that they felt a little guilty about not owning up to their part in the fiasco.

At least my conscience was clear. I finally learned a valuable lesson about going along with a crowd and began to think twice about doing so afterwards.

HUCK AND TOM RAFT AGAIN

In sixth grade I palled around with a classmate, Dave Morgan, during lunch period and on the playground. We became good friends, but didn't get the chance to go to each other's houses. He lived on the other side of Elbridge on Kingston Road. There was no way Mom or Dad would let me bike that far. Besides, one of the roads to his place was very busy and had lots of twists and turns where I could get clobbered by a car cutting a corner.

After talking about Dave at the supper table for a few weeks and hinting about him either coming to our place or me going to his, Mom said she'd give Mrs. Morgan a call.

Arrangements were made for me to go to Dave's house because Mrs. Morgan couldn't bring Dave to our place.

Dave and I talked about the coming Saturday when Mom would drive me to his place after dropping Dad off in Weedsport at O'Hara's Meat Market.

We were both excited about doing something together other than what little we could do together in school.

Mom left Terry in charge of the kids and picked me up when she got back from Weedsport. When we got there, Mom got out of the car with me and talked to Mrs. Morgan about a pick-up time.

She didn't leave without saying to me, "Keep your nose clean, watch your manners, and I want you to be in one piece when I pick you up."

"Okay, Mom," I said in my most reassuring tone of voice.

She still looked a little worried as she got back into the car and drove out of the driveway.

Dave showed me the cow barn and introduced me to his father, who was busy working on a broken hay bailer and didn't have much to say to us.

"Let's go out front and swing on the rope." Dave said as he started walking back towards the house with me right behind him.

A very long, thick rope hung from a big branch in the maple tree. We had a great time pushing each other and had many near misses with the rough barked trunk of the tree.

As Dave was giving me a big push he said, "Remember when I told you about the pond out back and the raft I built? How would you like to go back there and check it out?"

"That sounds like a great idea." I said as I dragged my sneakers on the ground to stop the swing.

We both raced part of the way and walked the rest, because the pond was a good distance behind the barn and it was a very warm day.

We went through a thick hedgerow where Dave had cut an opening and came upon a huge pond. It even had an island in the middle!

The cattails were think all around the pond. As we walked in the direction of the raft, frogs were constantly jumping into the water when we got close to them. The constant sounds of frogs, crickets, and flying insects made a pleasant, soothing sound when blended together.

We jumped back twice when huge water snakes came slithering across the path in front of us heading towards the water and safety. Both of us had heard enough snakes going through grass in the past to instantly recognize the sound and to be on guard.

The raft was a thing of beauty. It was made from several dead trees tied together with rope. I noticed a long pole sitting on top of it.

Dave said, "What do you think of it?"

"It's really grand. How did you build it?"

Dave replied, "My dad helped me haul the logs into the shallows, showed me how to tie them together, and let me go at it by myself."

"How long did it take you to finish the job?" I asked.

"Not that long. Maybe a couple of weeks." Dave said with pride.

"Can both of us get on it?" I asked hinting that I was dying to try it out.

"I don't know. The water almost comes over the top of the logs when I get on it."

"Do you think we could try?" I asked in an almost pleading tone.

"I guess so. But I will have to do the poling."

We took off our sneakers and socks, put them on the bank, and rolled up our pant legs.

I watched as Dave stepped onto the raft close to its center line. The raft went down some and the water was just about coming up through the logs.

"Step where I stepped. We will have to center our weight so we don't tip it over." Dave said with a hint of seriousness in his voice.

"Okay." I said as I gingerly got onto the raft.

It immediately had water a few inches over the top of the logs.

"I think it will work," Dave said and continued, "You stay where you are and I'll use the pole to back us out of the shallow water."

I found that if I spread my legs and bent my knees, I could adjust my weight from one side to the other to counter Dave's poling.

"When we were about thirty feet from shore, I said, "How deep is it here?"

"A good six feet," Dave said with no concern at all in his voice.

Six feet! A guy could drown in six feet of water!

Dave read my mind and said, "Don't worry. If we fall off we can grab onto the raft and use our feet to kick us back to shore."

I relaxed some and said, "Let's pretend we are pirates looking for treasure."

"Good idea." Dave returned.

I started using the gravelly voice I heard Long John Silvers use on <u>Treasure Island</u>. Dave got caught up in our pretending and used what he thought was a pirate voice. We started talking about walking the plank, boarding sailing ships, and pillaging the passengers onboard them.

Before we got to the island, we boarded at least three ships and had our imaginary treasure chest filled with gold and silver.

Once we hit dry land, Dave and I got off the raft and pretended to lug our treasure chest to its hiding place. This was rather difficult because the island had tall grass growing all over it. We solved the problem by stomping down some of the grass as a pretend way of digging a hole. After lowering our treasure chest and burying it, we went back to the raft.

Neither one of us noticed that a good breeze had picked up while we were burying our treasure and would be coming right at us as Dave poled the raft back to its landing spot.

The return voyage seemed to take forever. Our progress was very slow and Dave was quickly running out of steam.

"Dave, do you want me to take over?" I said. "I've been watching how you pole and think I can handle it."

If Dave wasn't so tired, I'm sure he would have said no. Instead he said, "Alright. But be careful and don't capsize us."

The pirate voices had long ago disappeared. Now our only goal was to get back to shore.

Dave handed me the pole and I started gingerly poling. I soon learned not to lean too far back after almost going in. It took several minutes to get the hang of it and keep us in a relatively straight line. The wind was fighting us all the way, and the landing spot seemed to get ever so slowly closer.

I was in a good lather by the time the raft hit shore. We jumped off and tied the raft to a small tree close to the edge of the water. Dave and I looked at each other and smiled in a way that showed we had beaten death.

We didn't say much as we put our socks and sneakers back on and walked back to the house because neither of us had enough energy left in us to walk and talk at the same time. Sprawled out on the grass in the front yard, we caught our breath and got some of our energy back.

Mrs. Morgan fixed us a big, farmer's lunch. Afterwards we were too stuffed to do much of anything, so we hung around the barn and played in the hayloft.

I was surprised to see Mom pulling into the driveway because the time went by so quickly, except when we were poling against the wind.

I made sure to thank Mrs. Morgan and Dave for having me over and got into the car. Once in the car, I chattered away about what Dave and I did, but left out the part about our journey back to the mainland.

Mom said, "It sounds like you had a grand adventure. Which one of you was Huck Finn, and who was Tom Sawyer?"

"I don't know, Mom. I never thought about them today. Dave and me were too busy having our own adventures."

CHUBBY TROUT

Somebody told me, I can't for the life of me remember who it was, that he caught a mess of trout just up from Cowels Chemical Company. I didn't really believe him because I knew nothing could or did live in the creek down by our street. I was getting desperate to catch something bigger than a four inch bullhead in Sheldon Pond with the strong possibility of it giving me a sting worse than any hornet could, so I thought I'd give it a try.

Early one morning before the sun got itself up and frying me even a deeper red than I already was, I dug up a can of earthworms from our garden, gathered my meager fishing gear together and started out. To save time, I took the shortcut behind Waterbury Felt and was soon scouting out a potential fishing spot just above the chemical plant. My fishing spots seemed very limited because of the bushes and thick mud along most of the bank. The only fishing spot I saw was almost straight down from the railroad tracks.

I slowly sidestepped down the loose stones and cinders to a narrow, flat spot between the bottom of the railroad bed and the water. After I put my gear down, I rigged up the huge hook with a worm. I used a huge hook because I figured that the bigger the hook, the bigger the fish I could catch.

Before I cast the rig into the creek, I checked out both sides of the water and in between for things that could snag my line. A willow tree was to my left and had a good sized branch leaning almost all the way across the creek with its far end submerged in the water. To my right, a bush had branches growing out into and above the water. Straight ahead looked like clear sailing, but I didn't know for sure because I could not see through the muddy water.

On my first cast, I snagged a hidden branch. I hauled it in, threw it out of the way, and cast again. This time I reeled the line in a bit and didn't feel anything grabbing onto my hook, so I let it be.

I stood there holding my pole waiting for a monster to bite down onto the hook. It didn't happen, so I looked out across the water at the swampy area beyond. The land was just above the water and was covered with cattails. I knew it would be impossible to stand on it even if I had a way to get across the twenty foot stretch of water.

I was brought back from various thoughts when I felt a slight tug on my line. I waited. A stronger tug came. I quickly yanked the end of my pole up and began reeling in the line. The fish didn't put up much of a fight and was quickly landed onto the narrow beach.

I examined it carefully to see if it was a trout. It didn't have any scales and was shaped something like the trout I had caught with Uncle Jimmy.

Deciding that it must be some type of trout I wasn't familiar with, I kept it. I found a long stick and slid the fish onto it through its gill. I then stuck the stick into the water to keep the fish alive for a bit.

The fishing was great. I used up all the worms in the can and walked home with ten or so trout on the stick. The fish were all dead by the time I proudly announced my return to Mom and showed her the fish.

"My, you sure got a mess of them," she said while looking them over.

"Are they trout, Mom?" I asked.

She held them up close to her eyes and said, "They don't look like any trout I ever saw around here or in England, but they don't have scales. The only other fish I know that don't have them besides trout are bullhead and catfish, so I guess they are trout."

Mom added, "Do you want me to fry them up for lunch?"

"Sure. That would be grand." I said.

"Have you ever cleaned a fish, Michael?"

"No, Mom. Can you clean them for me?" I said with a bit of pleading in my voice.

"Nonsense! I'll show you how to do it. Then you can do the rest," she said and went on, "Come out back with me."

We went to the top of the hill and stopped.

"Give me a fish," she said as she was taking her ever-present Camillus pocket knife out of her apron pocket.

She put the fish on a small board she had retrieved from the barn and cut off its head. Next she slit its belly from the business end all the way up to where the head used to be attached. She then got some fingers inside the opening and cleaned out its guts.

"Now it's your turn to try," she said as the knife went from her hand to mine.

I hesitated a split second before I cut a head off. I hesitated even longer before I slit the belly open and ripped out the guts.

"Good job. Make sure to rinse out all the little pieces of gut under the garden hose. I'll get you something to put them in."

Each time I cleaned one, it became easier to do, but it still took me a long time to finish the job. After rinsing them off, I took them into the kitchen.

Mom put the fish into a bowl of water and added salt.

"I'll let them sit for a bit in the salty water and rinse them off again. Then I can fry them up for you."

I washed my smelly hands and hung around the kitchen talking to Mom about my little fishing trip.

"It makes sense that you caught something above the chemical company. All the stuff they dump in there sure doesn't flow upstream." She said as she rinsed the fish, rolled them in batter, and began putting them into a hot frying pan.

They smelled really good as they sizzled and spit in the pan and my mouth was beginning to water. My brothers and sisters were in the house and were drawn to the smell. There were many sets of eyes looking at the fish as Mom carried the frying pan over to the table.

"Do you guys want to try some?" I asked, already knowing what the answer would be.

Mom piped in, "I'll have to take the meat off the bones. I don't want any of you choking to death on a fishbone."

Mom skillfully peeled off the meat by using a fork held backwards in her hand. All that was left were fish skeletons with tails still attached.

We sat down and ate the fish together. We all thought it tasted delicious except for little Peggy who said, "This tastes funny," as she spit out a mouthful onto her plate.

Mom thought it was okay but said it didn't taste like any trout she had ever eaten.

There wasn't enough fish to fill us, so Mom topped off our lunch with peanut butter and jelly sandwiches.

When Dad came home from work, I proudly told him about the fish I had caught.

"That's great! Where did you catch them?"

"In the creek just up from Cowels." I responded.

The smell of cooked fish was still in the air and Dad said in a serious tone already knowing the answer, "You didn't eat them, did you?"

"Everyone but Peggy and Maureen," I said. Maureen was just a baby and hadn't yet eaten anything more solid than a banana.

"It's a wonder that you all didn't get sick," he said with concern in his voice. He continued, "From now on, you can fish in the creek but don't eat anything from it."

I could see that Dad was upset as I said, "Yes, sir."

He then walked over to Mom and whispered something to her. I couldn't catch the drift of what he was saying. All I really heard was "keep an eye…"

He turned back to me and said, "Michael, those were creek chubs you caught. I don't want you eating anything from those waters ever again. Do you understand?"

Dad's tone and the way he looked at me with a serious expression told me much more than words ever could, and I answered with another, "Yes, sir."

For the rest of the evening, I could tell Mom and Dad were checking on us. I'd seen them in the past looking at us that way after one or two of the clan had been taken down with some powerful sickness to see if it was going to strike someone else.

I kept doing an inner examination of myself. Every little twinge experienced out of the ordinary was noted.

None of us got sick. I think the power of prayer and our strong constitutions saved us from the chemically altered fish.

WINTER AT SHELDON POND

The word quickly spread through the "kid vine" that the bigger kids had shoveled off the snow from ice-covered Sheldon Pond and were skating and playing hockey.

A year or so earlier, Uncle Jimmy gave me an old, beat up pair of hockey skates he had used in his younger years. I thanked him for giving them to me and took them home. They were too big, so I just put them in the back entrance room and forgot about them.

I never tried skating but heard it was fun once you got the hang of it and stopped constantly landing hard on the ice.

With the word out about Sheldon Pond, I dug out the skates and tried them on. I had huge feet for my age and the skates were just a bit too big for me. I tried an extra pair of heavy socks over the ones I already had on and the skates became a fairly close match to my feet.

When I told Mom what I wanted to do and added that older kids were there to make sure I stayed out of trouble, she said I could go.

Trudging through the deep snow in the field with the skates over my shoulder, I made it to the pond with some wind left in my lungs. I looked around to see about twenty kids spanning various ages playing hockey or just skating around. The older kids had a campfire burning for those who had cold feet or bodies that needed to be thawed on the same small, sandy beach I had used as a fishing spot in warmer weather.

I quickly got my boots off and started putting the skates on. Lacing them up took some doing, and my hands were pretty cold by the time I finally slipped my gloves back on.

Standing up on the skates was no problem because I was on snow. Once I hit the slight slope next to the ice, my troubles began. I fell several times trying to get down the little slope and finally decided that the best way to get onto the ice was to crawl out onto it like a baby.

I was getting very frustrated because when I tried to stand up, my feet kept coming out from under me.

Davey came skating up to me as if he was born on the things and said, "Here, let me give you a hand."

"Thanks," I said.

Once up, I noticed that my ankles kept going every which way. Davey gave me a slight push. I was off and gliding for a good five feet before my rump hit the ice.

Davey was patient with me and stuck around until I finally mastered getting up by myself. Then he was off to join in a hockey game.

I finally reached the point where I could stay up long enough to move by pushing off with one foot. Steering and stopping were completely out of the question, and I ran into rough spots in the ice with arms flaying. Thud!

Soon I learned to judge how much I should push off to get a glide going to get me just close enough to a rough area without running into it. I then did a slow ten or so point turn to another direction and started all over again.

I was concentrating so much on what I was doing that I couldn't see what the others were up to. My feet were getting very cold, so I decided to head back to shore to warm up by the fire.

I stood close enough to the fire to watch the snow slowly melt from the skates and made small talk with the kids standing around. We were all in the same boat when it came to skating. We exchanged stories of falls and possible techniques that might help us do better. We also watched the good skaters with awe and noted what they did.

Armed with hints from each other and from what we saw, we all got back onto the ice.

I pushed off with one foot and stopped myself by dragging a toe on the ice. It worked but I dug in too deeply and went down in a split. It hurt.

By the time I was getting too tired to skate any longer, I could push off using either skate and stop myself, but I couldn't make any good turns. I had to go in a giant half circle to get myself facing back to where I had come from.

A few of us walked home together just before it started to get dark. We all vowed to do better the next time we came.

I got better at skating with each trip to the pond and was even picked to help fill a hockey team. The older kids would go zooming by and the well-worn hockey puck had to come right at me before I could take a swing at it with a stick. There was no way I could chase after it and get it. (Only a few of the boys had hockey sticks, the rest of us picked up long sticks that were left on shore to use.)

We had a chance to catch our breath when the hockey puck went sailing off the ice and into the deep snow because it took time to dig it out. A great celebration was held after a team scored a goal by getting the puck past the goalie and between the two rocks placed on the ice behind him.

By the time the big spring thaw came, I could move around the ice without falling too much or running over some little kid.

I hoped that I'd remember some of the things I learned about skating by the time Sheldon Pond froze over again next winter.

BENDING BRANCHES

Sheldon Pond thawed and it was late winter. I was in seventh grade and still pining a bit about Mary Cotter moving to the Skaneateles School District. (Mary was my first love, but she never knew about it.) I was sitting in English class following along in my book while the teacher read poetry. I hated poetry with a passion and thought it to be girl stuff. The teacher finished up a section with a poem about a girl with flowers in her hair and started telling us about Robert Frost. After she read about him being raised in New England and said how great a poet he was, she had us turn to a poem titled "Bending Branches."

I thought to myself, "Here we go again!"

The more the teacher read, the more I liked the poem. By the time she was finished, I liked the guy. I also wanted to try bending my own branches.

I knew exactly where to find saplings that might be good to experiment on and got right down to business once I got off the bus, changed, and finished my chores.

It was a fairly warm day with the temperature a bit above freezing, so I didn't have to wear much more than a light jacket, gloves, hat, and boots.

The saplings that held promise were almost in front of the McEneny house and close to the ruins of the burned out button factory.

I got to the spot and checked out the trees. Most of them were about five inches in diameter at the bottom and went straight up a good thirty feet. They had just a few branches here and there that could be used to get me high up into them.

Climbing one wasn't that hard. In spots I had to shimmy up short distances to reach other branches. I could tell when I was high enough because the tree started swaying a foot or so to the side when I leaned out a little.

I knew the hard parts for me were going to be getting up courage to lean out far enough and releasing my feet from the tree, while keeping a good grip on the trunk with my hands.

I started swaying back and forth until I was swinging three or four feet out to either side. It was great fun, but I wasn't bending branches the way the boy did in the poem.

I finally got up the nerve to unwrap my legs from the tree after I got myself way out on a good sway. The sapling slowly bent down. I let my hands go free of the tree when I was only a few feet off the ground.

What great fun! What a thrill!

I immediately went back up the same tree and did it again and again.

After the fourth trip down, I noticed that the sapling was loosing its spring and I was coming down quicker. I chanced another try and came down fast enough to have my feet hit the frozen ground pretty hard.

I watched the sapling slowly go back up. It didn't return to its original position and had a decent bow in it.

Deciding that it wouldn't be safe to use that sapling again, I found another one nearby and bent it until I figured it was no longer safe to use anymore.

My arms were tired. I didn't want to quit, but didn't have the strength to climb another tree,.

I went home feeling happy about what I had done.

"Where have you been, Michael?" Mom asked.

"I was across the road climbing some small trees," I said. I didn't dare tell Mom what I was doing once I had climbed them.

"How high up were you going?"

"No more than fifteen to twenty feet," I said as if it wasn't any great height at all and giving a hint that I had climbed much higher into trees at other times.

"Well, you just be careful. I don't want you limping around here with a cast on your leg, or even worse, seeing you in a casket at O'Neill's Funeral Home." She said the last part as a special effect to scare me away from being foolish.

"Yes, Mom. I'll be careful. I won't be climbing any big trees." I said it thinking about how good I was getting at using words like lawyers on television did.

I was anxious to try bending branches the next day and couldn't wait for school to end.

As usual, the school day dragged because I had something special planned. To top it off, I had several extra chores to do before I could get myself headed in the direction I wanted to be going.

It was much colder than it was the previous day, but I didn't want to get all bundled up. It would make it very hard to climb the saplings.

I tried to sneak out with what I had worn the day before, but Mom caught me.

"You get yourself back in here this instant, young man, and get your winter coat on."

Heck. I almost had the door closed behind me when she said this.

I got my winter coat on and went to the saplings.

It was much harder climbing wearing the bulky coat, but I managed. The first tree was a good one, and I got at least five rides down on it before my feet started hitting too hard to bend it anymore.

Feeling pretty cocky about my new-found talent, I looked around for the tallest sapling. It had several good branches, and I was close to the top before I looked down. The ground sure looked a lot further away than it did from the tops of the other trees I had bent.

My cockiness was greater than my fear, so I started swaying the tall sapling back and forth. When I got into what I thought was a good enough sway, I let go with my feet and slowly started down. I was still far from the ground when I heard the sapling cracking. Before it could completely register in my brain what was happening, I was falling to the ground with the broken top of the tree held firmly in my hands.

My feet hit very hard and the wind got knocked completely out of my sails. It seemed like an hour before I could suck in any air and tears of pain began to well up in my eyes. It took me some time before I got slowly to my feet. I was sore all over and couldn't walk without limping.

After hobbling around and checking various regions of my body for broken parts and finding none, I slowly headed for home.

I looked through the window to make sure the coast was clear before I entered the kitchen and went into the bathroom to check myself out for any damage. The only visible hurt was a good-sized welt just below my right shin.

As I got my clothes back on, I counted my blessings and thanked God for sparing me once again.

I thought about what had happened and used my limited science knowledge to finally decide that the cold air had made the sapling brittle.

My bending branches days were over, but I still liked Robert Frost. I never completely understood "Mending Fences" and didn't bother to go looking for any to fix.

THE SHERIDAN BOYS

The Waltons had moved again. They now lived in the small Hamlet of Mandana about six miles down on the west side of Skaneateles Lake. Their house was empty, a for sale sign was up, and the noise level in Stump City went down by about half.

I made friends with Danny and Corky Sheridan. They lived on Phillips Street and went to Skaneateles School. The school district line between Skaneateles and Elbridge ran down the center of Phillips Street. Since they lived on the south side of the line, they had to go to Skaneateles.

Because of this and their being a few years younger than me, it took a long time before I really got to know them. I'd see them around and they'd join in community games, like playing softball or huge capture the flag contests.

It was a gradually growing friendship—developed by playing at either my house or theirs. It got to the point where we were seeing each other almost everyday.

The only drawbacks were my two sisters, Terry and Pat. They both took a liking to Danny and Corky, so they interrupted our playing by just being around.

It annoyed me much more than it annoyed Danny and Corky. I even got the idea that they liked having my sisters hanging around with us.

Who could like my sisters?

If we got lucky, we were able to play in the Tehan twins' sandbox. The Tehan kids were much younger than we were and had the huge sandbox in their backyard next door to the Sheridan house.

We'd spend hours building roads, bridges, and tunnels. The only bad thing about it was some cat liked to use it too. We had to be careful and get rid of what the cat left behind before we started playing.

The best thing about the Sheridan boys was they never teased me like the older kids did. They didn't pick on me because of my red hair and freckled face, and I never felt defensive around them.

It's good to have friends who like you for who you are and don't find just enough fault to make you feel uneasy.

BUS RACING

I couldn't wait to get my bike out of the shed. It had been stored in there collecting dust since the snow started to fly in early November and the roads became too icy to ride on.

The day came when the weather looked like the snow season was finally over and it would be safe to get back into "bike shape." I got the bike out and started working on it. It took some time to pump up the tires, oil the chain and other moving parts, adjust the brake, and clean off the grime.

I took it for a test spin up and down the street. It worked just fine, so I went all around Stump City and ventured over to the Falls section for a longer ride.

In a week or so, my legs and wind were conditioned, and I got itching to travel beyond the community boundaries. I got up the courage to ask Mom if I could bike to school instead of riding on the bus.

She said she'd think about it. This surprised me because I was expecting an instant "no" from her.

I learned long ago not to pester either Mom or Dad about something, so I kept my mouth shut and waited.

A few days later I got back from a ride and put the kickstand down. Mom was outside working on her flower bed—she always loved doing something outside, especially working with flowers.

"Where did you ride to today, Michael?" She asked as she wiped off some dirt she saw on her apron.

"I just went up to Danny's house. We were playing fetch with Brighty until his tongue was almost hanging down to the ground."

Mom smiled and said, "Brighty is a good dog. I've always liked Irish setters."

She bent back down, quickly pulling weeds from around a rose bush and said, "I talked it over with your father. It's okay if you ride your bike to school. But, you must stop at all the stop signs and look out for traffic. Okay?"

I smiled as I said, "I'll be very careful, Mom."

Mom suddenly got the very far away look in her eyes when she was about to talk or was thinking about her life in England.

She said, "I rode my three speed English bike all over the place. Not many people could afford to buy cars and later on the War brought on gas rationing. I didn't think anything about biking five miles up and down the hills."

"Did you ever get tired out?" I asked.

"Only if the trip was extra long. Riding bikes was the way most folks in the English countryside got from one place to another. In the big cities they had trams and tubes."

She stood back, looked me directly in the eyes and said, "Every so often a bicyclist would get clobbered by a car or truck and end up either dead or in the hospital."

To reassure her I said, "I promise to be careful."

Since the bus had to take the long way to school up Stump Road and then down Vinegar Hill Road, I decided to leave for school at the same time it picked up the kids in Stump City.

I found it to be an easy ride because most of it was downhill. I made sure to stop at every stop sign and got way over to the right to let the few passing cars go by me. My bus didn't get to school until long after I had put my bike in the bike stand in front of the building. This gave me a big thrill.

I thought about the ride home during the day and knew I was in for a hard go of it. The toughest hill was just outside the Village of Elbridge. I made it about half way up before I couldn't pedal any further. I got off and walked the rest of the way to the top. I didn't even get close to Hartlot before my bus passed me. Some of the kids saw me, so they waved and shouted out the open windows. Some were shouting friendly things and a few were yelling things like, "Quigley, get a horse!"

This upset me. Right then and there, I made a vow to myself that one of these days I'd beat the bus back to Stump City.

I pedaled to school on the days the weather was good in the morning and not threatening to rain in the afternoon. Soon I was able to pedal all the way to the top of the steep hill just outside of Elbridge at the beginning of my personal race against the bus and gained lots of ground on it.

Within two weeks, I was more than halfway home before the bus took the lead. Now the kids on the bus were cheering me on. This gave me an added boost to my vow to beat the bus to our stop.

The day finally came when I could steam my way almost to Rodak's Bar without being out of breath and my legs aching. It was on that day that I missed beating the bus by no more than a minute or so. The next day I went cruising by as it made its usual stop at the Tambroni house to let off half a dozen kids or so and knew I would win.

With a big grin on my face, I waited at our bus stop for it to come around the bend and over the creek. The kids were amazed at what I had done, and Mr. Hanville, a man who appreciated speed more than most, gave me a tip of his hat and a big smile when he opened the door to let the kids out.

Since I knew I now could beat the bus anytime I pleased, I sometimes took my time riding home and admired the scenery like a Sunday driver.

THE COLONIAL THEATRE

If Mom drove Dad to his Saturday job at O'Hara's Meat Market in Weedsport, and if she didn't have other plans, and if we were lucky, Mom would drive Terry, Pat, and me to Skaneateles for the Saturday Matinee at the Colonial Theatre.

The Colonial was located on the lake side of Genesee Street close to Thayer Park. The movie house had seen better days: Days before television entered almost every home in the area.

We paid our dime at the ticket booth, climbed up the stairs to the right, and entered a world of semi-wild kids making all kinds of noise before the lights went down and the screen came to life. My sisters found friends, and I did the same. We wouldn't see each other again until the matinee ended, which was fine and dandy with me.

Sam Dove was the protector of the realm and kid bouncer. He was a giant of a guy. He was a lot closer to seven feet than six and weighed at least three hundred pounds on one of his lighter days. He cruised up and down the aisles giving those who were making too much noise or goofing off too much THE LOOK. Once a kid received THE LOOK from Sam—the number of times predetermined by Sam's mood that day—he was escorted out without getting a refund. Kids made fun of Sam behind his back, but never when Sam was turned their way. I never heard Sam say anything to a kid. He just pointed at a victim, stared, and the kid got up with Sam right behind to make sure he left.

Once the show started, it quieted down to a dull roar. We always saw a mess of cartoons followed by a movie. After the movie, there was a break in the action while kids spent more money on snacks than it cost them to get into the theatre. I waited in line and usually spent a dime on a candy bar that cost me only a nickel at Cronaeur's General Store.

When the snack stand operator figured she had sold enough candy to make a decent profit for the day, the lights went on and off a few times, and we hurried back to our seats to watch more cartoons and another movie.

I was always quiet for the cartoons because I loved them. Sometimes I had a problem focusing on a movie that wasn't the greatest and got **The Look**, but never more than once.

The scariest movie I ever saw at the Colonial was **The Fly**. Vincent Price was the star. He was a frightening man just to look at without turning into a fly with a man's head. The suspense and scary scenes made the hair on the back of my neck stand on end. I wanted to close my eyes but couldn't. Kids screamed during the bad parts. I'm sure there were lots of kids who itched to run out, but didn't want to be called scaredy cats for the next month. When the movie ended and the lights came back up, the tension level in all of us dropped several notches.

Mom was either waiting for us when we got out, or we stayed in front of the theatre under the marquee until she came.

It was great fun going to a matinee, even when I had to peel some type of sticky candy from the bottom of my shoes or pants when we got home.

CLIFT PARK

On hot summer days when swimming lessons at Jordan Pool were finished for the summer, I sometimes got on my bike and pedaled to Skaneateles with Danny and Corky riding beside me. Of course, Terry and Pat also had to tag along to keep an eye on their loved ones. To their credit, my sisters didn't slow us down much, and the three or four mile ride didn't take very long.

We always parked our bikes in a spot where they wouldn't get stepped on, took off our shorts and shirts, and slowly got into the very cold water. There was no quick way to get all wet in a hurry because we first had to walk around the little kids in their play area without splashing them. We'd be just about up to our waists by the time we could finish getting the rest of our bodies wet. It was slow torture in the cold water.

The water got deep quickly. Anyone who wanted to go beyond the kiddy play area had to take a swimming test before he was allowed on or near the rafts anchored in the swimming area. The one closest to the seawall was called the little raft and the second one, the big raft, was a good hundred feet further out. To get on the little one, you had to first swim to it and back to the seawall while a lifeguard watched. To be allowed on the big raft, you had to swim all the way out to the big one from the seawall and back again. With all the swimming lessons my sisters and I took at Jordan Pool over the years, we didn't have any problem passing the test for the baby raft. I had more swimming lessons, so I didn't have a problem passing the test for the big raft.

The Sheridan boys didn't live in the Elbridge School District, so they didn't have swimming lessons. They didn't even bother to take the raft test. Terry and Pat kept the two boys company while I made several trips out to the big raft.

We always had a good time. Once in awhile we walked across the street and bought an ice cream bar at the stone block garage next to the Sherwood Inn.

The only part we didn't enjoy was the bike ride back to the Falls. If it was a very hot day, we all were covered with sweat by the time we made the trip back home.

If the Sheridan boys were busy doing something else and couldn't go with me, sometimes I hitchhiked up to Skaneateles to swim. I never had a problem getting a ride, usually with someone who lived in the area. It saved being all sweaty when I returned.

The only time a trip to the park by myself left a sour taste in my mouth happened when I got out of the water to take a short break in the shade. I was sitting on a towel minding my own business looking at the kids diving off the rafts when I heard something out of the ordinary happening over to my left. I turned and saw a short, muscular guy picking on three kids a few years younger than me.

I watched him poke and push them for a few seconds and my blood began to boil. Since I was picked on as a little kid, I knew exactly what they were going through and didn't like it one bit.

I got up off my towel and walked over to the scene.

"Why are you picking on these little kids?" I said with a hint of anger in my voice.

"It's none of your business, so butt out," hissed the bully.

I stepped between him and the little kids to show him I wasn't going to butt out.

Without any warning, he came at me with his fists bawled up and took a wild, hard swing at my face. I ducked as his fist barely grazed the top of my head. I cut loose a sharp left-hook to his chin that sent him back-pedaling until he tripped over a mound of clothing. (I would've hit him in the nose, but he was wearing glasses. I didn't want to break them and go through what I had gone through with Kevin.) He got up rubbing his chin and backed away a little more.

"Get out of here and leave the kids alone," I said in a measured tone I used to hide the fear I felt inside.

The bully backed away even more, turned, and quickly walked away.

As I started to walk back to my towel, one of the kids said, "Thanks."

On second thought, I guess it wasn't such a bad day at the park.

FROM BERRY PICKING TO WALKING THE PLANK

I was helping Dad hill the potatoes in the garden and was reminded of the sound Mrs. Wickham's hoe made as it sliced through the dirt.

Dad's hoe went silent. "Michael, I saw Mr. Caddy this morning. He needs pickers in his strawberry patch. How would you like to make some extra money? He's paying ten cents a quart."

He added this as a lure because he knew I liked to work for money.

I was almost hooked but thought about the size of the wild blackberries I picked along hedgerows and figured it would take at least an hour to pick a quart of them.

"Are they bigger than blackcaps?"

"Mr. Caddy said they are good sized and it shouldn't take long to pick a quart."

I was hooked. "When does he want me to start?"

"Tomorrow morning," Dad said.

"Okay, I'll ride down and pick some for him."

We went back to work in silence. Neither one of us wanted to waste energy talking when there were so many rows left to hill.

It was a short ride down County Line Road to Mr. Caddy's place. His trailer was on the corner of Irish and Taylor Road where he and his wife lived in the summer. Their main house was in Florida. His daughter, Mrs. Burke, lived in the big farm house close to the trailer.

A few kids were already picking in the patch. I recognized them from school and yelled a greeting.

Mr. Caddy, who had his back to me, was getting on in years, so he wasn't doing any picking. Besides, he was the boss of the operation and had to supervise the help. He was standing by the edge of the patch next to a stack of empty quart baskets.

He heard me, turned, and said, "Hello, Michael. I'm glad you could make it. I've got lots of ripe berries needing quick picking. I want to get them to market by eleven this morning."

"Yes, Mr. Caddy."

"Here's a stack of baskets. Come over with me, and I'll show you where to start."

I followed him to the beginning of a row.

"You can start here and work your way to the end. Then, come back up the next row. Fill the baskets just over the top and leave them on the ground. I'll pick them up and keep track of what you've picked. I'll settle up with you when you are done. I'm paying ten cents a quart. Does that sound good to you?"

I nodded and took the baskets from his outstretched hand.

As I was bending over to start, Mr. Caddy said, "Oh, you can eat all you want."

"Yes, sir!" I said with surprise.

What a deal! I'd not only get paid ten cents a quart to pick them, I could eat them too!

I squatted down and began picking. The first berry went straight into my mouth. It was delicious, so I had another and another. I had to will myself to start putting berries into the empty basket. I soon had a full belly and an almost empty basket and began to concentrate on filling the basket.

The more I picked, the better I got at it. I quickly learned that there were more berries than met the eye when I lifted up a bunch of berry leaves to retrieve an extra large one and found many hidden ones.

The squatting position didn't last long. I got down on my knees with the straw bedding around the plants acting like a nice cushion.

I was concentrating on my work and filled several baskets when I suddenly got startled.

"Mike, I'm glad you could make it," Mr. Caddy said.

I turned. Mr. Caddy wasn't looking in my direction. I followed his eyes to see him looking at Mike Burke, his grandson.

Mr. Caddy led Mike over to a spot a few rows over from me and said, "Mike, you know Michael Quigley, don't you?"

"We ride the same bus to school, Grandpa." Mike returned.

"Good. You can start on these two rows."

Mike said, "Yes, Grandpa."

We didn't say much to each other at first, but as time went by, we started talking about boy things.

Mike said, "Do you have a B.B. gun?"

"Sure do," I said.

"How would you like to come down sometime and shoot at pigeons?"

"Sounds like fun," I returned.

I decided that I liked Mike and looked forward to playing with him.

Before I finished picking my two rows, enough kids from the area arrived to cover the rest of the rows, so my part of the job was done for the day.

"I'll see you later," I said to Mike as I got up with my final quart and walked over to Mr. Caddy.

"I'll be here," Mike replied.

When I was getting closer to Mr. Caddy, he said, "Good job, Michael. Now let me see how many quarts you picked."

Mr. Caddy looked down at the paper attached to his clipboard, checked off the quarts by my name and said, "Very good, Michael. You got a whooping twelve quarts."

I grinned from ear to ear and knew it was good that I didn't keep on eating too many berries while I was picking.

As he pulled a silver dollar and two dimes out of his pants, he said, "I've got a few days of picking left on the patch. Do you plan on coming back to help me finish the job?"

"Sure thing, Mr. Caddy," I returned as he handed me the money.

I pedaled home, had a quick drink of water, got the Reo reel mower out, and left to cut Mr. Kimak's and Mr. Phillip's lawns. It turned out to be one of my biggest money-making days ever.

For the next two days I picked berries, and Mike always picked in the rows next to mine. We concentrated more on our picking than talking, but still got to know and like each other a bit better.

I made good money on the second day. By the third day the patch was getting thinner than the hair on Dad's head, so I only picked seven quarts.

As I was finishing up my last row, Mike asked me if I could come down with my B.B. gun the next morning. I said I would once I got my chores done.

I couldn't ride a bike and carry my B.B. gun at the same time, so I walked to Mike's place. I took the shortcut through Kimak's field to save some time and shot at things on the way pretending I was killing off assorted bad guys and monsters.

I knocked on the back door of Mike's huge farm house and Mrs. Burke answered. "Hello. You must be Michael," she said with a warm smile on her face. "Please come in."

I rested my B.B. gun on the door jam and she beckoned me into the kitchen. I waited there while she went to find Mike.

I couldn't believe the size of the kitchen. It was almost as big as the whole first floor in our house! It also had new-fangled appliances Mom talked about but could never afford nor have enough space in her kitchen to put them.

Mrs. Burke retuned to the kitchen and said, "Mike will be right in. How's your Mom doing?"

"She's fine Mrs. Burke," I replied.

"That's good. Did you know that I've known your father since I was a little girl?"

"No, I didn't." I said this with a look that showed I wanted to know more.

"Your Dad would help me with some of my chores when he worked on my father's farm."

I should have made the connection earlier but didn't.

Mike came into the kitchen with his Daisy B.B. gun and said, " Hi, Mike. Are you ready to go hunting?"

"Sure am!" I said.

"Now, you two be careful and don't shoot at the cats." Mrs. Burke warned as we were going out the door.

As we walked to the now abandoned huge barns to the back and side of the house, Mike said, "Maybe we can sneak up on some rats in the barn before we go into the upper part to shoot at pigeons."

Instantly we both crouched down and walked as quietly and slowly as two boys are capable of doing.

We entered the barn and were in the area where the cows had once been put during milking times and when the weather was bad for them to be outside.

"Look, down there!" Mike whispered as he pointed.

Sure enough, a small rat was knawing something by the far wall.

Mike said, "Go ahead and take a shot."

I slowly raised the Red Rider, aimed high because I had learned that the greater the distance to a target, the more the B.B. dropped, and squeezed the trigger.

The rat jumped a good two feet into the air and quickly disappeared.

"Nice shot. You hit him!" Mike said with surprise.

"Thanks." I said sounding like I hit my target every time I fired my gun.

We walked around the lower part for awhile longer but didn't see any more rats.

"Let's go upstairs and check it out for critters." Mike said.

I followed him up the steep stairs to what used to be the hayloft. There was still some hay and a bit of straw left on the floor. Much of the space was loaded with old farm equipment which had long been out of use because all of it had to be pulled by horses. The equipment was covered with a thick layer of dust and pigeon droppings. There was even a fancy looking horse sleigh that could carry six people.

Way up on the rafters we could see a few dozen pigeons perched and cooing. They looked like they were all on the alert.

As soon as Mike raised his gun to his shoulder, all of them took off through a broken window by the roof peak.

"Darn, I haven't had a good shot in ages. I think they've been stung too many times with B.B. shot."

I followed Mike and went through a small opening between the two huge sliding doors and down the dirt ramp.

"Hey! I've got a good idea!" Mike said.

"What is it?" I replied.

Let's go to the silo and check it out."

"Sounds good to me," I replied.

The silo was at the end of one of the barns. It was round, made out of concrete, and had a wooden roof.

I followed Mike through the small opening at its base. I looked straight up and couldn't believe how tall it was. The floor was covered with old, moldy chopped corn with a thin top layer of pigeon droppings.

I noticed a plank running from one side to the other when we first looked up and wondered what it was used for and how someone got it up there to begin with.

"It sure is a long way up," I said.

Mike answered with a hint of boasting, "I've climbed to the top before."

"Really?" I returned.

"Sure have. I've done it loads of times. Pigeons have nests up there. I wanted to get some little ones and raise them, but the nests were empty at the time. I think they might be nesting now."

"It would be fun to raise pigeons." I said.

"Do you want to climb to the top and see if any are there?" Mike said.

I looked at the round metal rungs going straight up the side and said, "I don't know. That's a long way to climb."

"Ah, come on. If I can do it, you sure can." Mike said.

I noticed a tinge of "What are you—a chicken?" in his tone.

Mike was almost two years younger than me, and it sure wouldn't look good around the neighborhood if word got out that I was too afraid to climb a silo that a kid much younger than me had climbed.

As bravely as I could, I said, "Okay. Hold my gun."

I slowly went up making sure I had a good grip on the next rung and looked down to make sure my feet were in good spots before I moved up to the next one.

As I carefully continued, Mike kept yelling to me, "You're doing great."

I certainly didn't feel as confident as he did, but I kept going.

When I finally reached the top, I looked down and focused my eyes for the first time on the bottom. It even seemed higher than it did when I was looking up from ground level. Mike's upturned head looked very small.

I took some deep breaths to quiet the shaking in my body.

"Do you see any nests up there?"

I looked around and without thinking said, "Yes. There's one on the other side, but I can't tell if there's anything in it."

"Go across the plank until you can see if it's empty or not." Mike said as if it wasn't out of the ordinary to go across the narrow board at the top of the silo.

I didn't think fast enough and say something like, "Oh, I got a better look. It's empty," before I started inching my way across the narrow plank.

Every time I crawled a bit further out onto the plank, it went up and down a little more. By the time I got out near the middle, it had a slight bow in it. Now I not only had to worry about falling off, I had to worry about the plank breaking!

When I was just passed the middle, I looked over at the nest and saw that it was empty. At least I was spared going all the way across and then figuring out a way to carry birds back down with me.

"It's empty." I tried to sound disappointed.

I then slowly went backwards on the plank and made it to the end without killing myself.

Going back down the rungs wasn't bad at all. The closer I got to the bottom, the quicker I went and the bigger Mike's head became.

Hitting solid ground sent a wave of relief going through my body. Without thinking, I wiped the sweat from my brow and let out a deep breath. Did Mike notice I had been afraid?

"I can't believe you went across the plank. I was too scared to do it, and I didn't know if the plank would hold." Mike said.

"You never went across the plank?" I said with utter disbelief.

"Heck, no," he quickly said and went on, "Please don't tell my mom or dad or anybody else that I went to the top."

"Okay. Just as long as you don't tell my mom or dad what I did." I returned.

"Deal." Mike quickly said.

We spent the rest of the morning out in the field shooting at leaves, golden rod stems, and big insects.

We were just about out of ammo when Mike's mom called him in for lunch.

I walked over to the house with him and thanked him and his mom for having me over.

She said, "You're welcome anytime, Michael."

I then said so long to Mike and headed for home.

On the way back, I didn't shoot at anything. I was too deep in thought. It dawned on me that it wasn't worth being killed to avoid being called a chicken.

The silo incident had put me much too close to meeting my Maker.

CONFUSING TIMES

Over the past year, when I was between thirteen and fourteen, I heard bits and pieces of conversations between Mom and Dad about moving to a bigger house.

I had to admit that it was getting a little cramped. There were now seven of us kids. Six of us were in one bedroom with a curtain running down the center to make a girl side and a boy side, and little Peg was sleeping on a steamer trunk at the end of the curtain. Grandma Simpson was in the tiny room at the top of the stairs. Mom and Dad had baby Maureen, who was going on two, in their bedroom.

It would be nice to live in a bigger house, but I didn't really want to move out of Stump City. Good friends were hard to come by. I didn't want to lose the ones I had and have to start all over again finding new ones.

I wasn't surprised when Mom and Dad gathered us all together and announced that they were in the process of buying a bigger house, but I wasn't prepared for the news either.

After church on the Sunday following their announcement, we all piled into the 57 Chevy and went to see our future home. We kids were all amazed at the size of it. It was bigger than just about any home in Stump City, but needed lots of work.

Dad said that it would take a few months before all the paper work was done and we could move in, so I tried to block out the move as much as I could.

I played with my friends more often than usual, and we promised to visit each other once I moved. None of us knew if this would be true, but we hoped it would be.

Reality hit me about moving when the school year ended and we only had a month before we left Stump City. I made arrangements with one friend to take over my mowing jobs, told Big Jim McEneny that he'd have to find someone to go to Cronaeur's Store for his supplies, and handed over my <u>TV Guide</u> route to another friend.

Doing all these things cemented the move in my mind. I was resigned to it and filled with doubts.

Right after Mom and Dad signed the papers to close the deal on the house, things rapidly changed. All of us old enough to pull our weight were given jobs to do at the new house. The girls concentrated on cleaning up the inside while I helped Dad do the many repairs needed to be completed before we could move in.

It was at least a week of getting up in the morning and then going to the new house to work most of the day. I was slowed down for a few days when I drank water from a bathroom faucet in the new house and became very sick.

The final days in Stump City were a blur of activity and my good-byes weren't what I wanted them to be.

When I watched Dad turn the key to lock the door on our house, it was if a door was closing on almost thirteen years of my life.

Could I ever go back to Stump City again? I didn't know, but maybe, just maybe I could crack the front door a little bit and take a quick peek back inside when I got older.